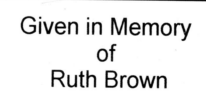

Little Visits at Bedtime

105 Devotions and Prayers

Dr. Mary Manz Simon

Illustration by Ed Koehler

CONCORDIA PUBLISHING HOUSE • SAINT LOUIS

Published 2012 by Concordia Publishing House
3558 S. Jefferson Avenue, St. Louis, MO 63118-3968
1-800-325-3040 • www.cph.org

Manufactured in China.
Heshan, China/047365/300382

Library of Congress Cataloging-in-Publication Data

Simon, Mary Manz, 1948–
  Little visits at bedtime / Mary Manz Simon.
    p. cm.
  ISBN 978-0-7586-3442-9
  1. Families—Prayers and devotions. 2. Children—Prayers and devotions.
  3. Bedtime prayers. I. Title

BV255.S577 1995
249—dc23

2012005325

1 2 3 4 5 6 7 8 9 10   21 20 19 18 17 16 15 14 13 12

This book is dedicated to
Solomon Anwar Simon

I will not leave you as orphans; I will come to you. John 14:18

About This Book

Bedtime is eagerly anticipated by parents and just as eagerly postponed by young children. However, regardless of how exhausting or exciting a day has been, we all need restful sleep.

Routines or traditions can provide a helpful framework during the transition to bedtime. For example, before beginning to read from this book, you might say aloud a simple prayer:

Good night, God, it's time to sleep,
Tucked in bed so soft and deep.
Please watch over me this night
As I sleep till morning light.

Once your child hears that rhythmic verse, he will know it's time to settle down.

Use *Little Visits® at Bedtime* to help your family make a peaceful transition from busy day to peaceful night as you focus your thoughts and conversations on the blessings of your day and on God's gifts to you.

About Each Devotion

- These stories are not dated. That means if you miss a night, you can simply pick up where you left off.
- To personalize these stories, substitute the names of your child and his friends for names used in the book.
- Questions that follow each story often ask for creative thinking. Regardless of how your child responds, use her answers to extend your conversation.
- When you expand the prayer to include items of importance to your child, he is reminded that God listens to the concerns of our hearts.

Little Visits AT BEDTIME

Let's Remember
Call to Me and I will answer you.
Jeremiah 33:3

Who Will Be My Friend?

Dear God,

Parent Connection

Bringing It Home

Let's Talk

About Bedtime Routine

- Research shows that a regular bedtime routine has two positive outcomes: children fall asleep faster and awaken less frequently during the night. Some data also validates what parents know: a smooth bedtime improves the mood of the adults as well!
- Avoid the rush hour! If devotional time seems to be squeezed out of your family's schedule, then back into bedtime. Determine the actual time for "lights out," and then list all the activities that need to happen before you say good night. Add five minutes for inevitable stalling.

Table of Contents

7

Introduction

Bedtime is more than a bridge between day and night. For a child, sleepy-time conversations are an opportunity to review the day and share fears, hopes, and dreams. Shielded from the day's distractions, at bedtime, we recapture the purity of the parent-child relationship.

The brief talk-triggers in this book will help you and your child expand on both the big events and small details that define life. This time is invaluable because when we step back from the day, it is so simple to identify our many blessings. Of course, a child who is trying to delay the inevitable "lights out" will work hard to list every single person on the playground and recall many signs of God's goodness! But as your child remembers all that has filled the day, he comes to understand that God is truly with him, all the time and everywhere.

A little visit with God at bedtime transitions a child into a gentle close of the day as he "moves" from your loving arms to the comforting arms of his heavenly Father.

Mary Manz Simon

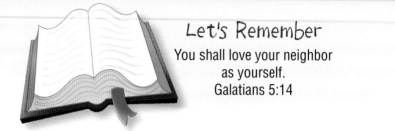

Let's Remember

You shall love your neighbor
as yourself.
Galatians 5:14

A Kind Friend

Abby headed across the playground to the slide. She giggled with her friends as they all raced to the ladder. Abby stopped abruptly before reaching the ladder. Zoey was on the first step, so Abby knew they didn't need to hurry. Zoey wore a brace on her leg. Just recently, she had started to go up and down the slide, but it took a very long time for Zoey to reach the top.

"Hey, who's the slow-poke?" said a voice behind Abby.

"We need to wait for Zoey," Abby explained, holding onto the ladder at the bottom of the stairs.

Girls in the back started to get restless. Soon, there was pushing and shoving.

"Move. Move!" Abby heard the voices behind her.

"We need to wait for Zoey," Abby repeated. "She's almost to the top, but she has to get off before we start climbing."

Abby felt children pushing against her, but she stood firm.

Let's Talk

Why couldn't Zoey climb faster? Why wouldn't Abby let the girls behind her push ahead? The Bible says we should be kind. How do you show kindness?

Parent Connection

Kindness is catching. Research shows that when someone receives kindness, that person passes it to another, another, and another. As a result, a single act of kindness can generate three more kind deeds. This is true not only in public situations, as when a person holds open a grocery store door, but in a family setting too. For years, family-life specialists have known instinctively that a child who lives with kindness learns kindness. Now this has been proven as a scientific fact.

Bringing It Home

• God showed His kindness to us while we were sinners by sending Jesus for us.

• God uses us to share His kindness with others.

Let's Remember
There is a time and a way for everything.
Ecclesiastes 8:6

Sun Time

Makayla loved to wander through her neighbor's yard. Makayla visited so often that she knew where the hose attachments were put away and where the watering can was stored. Makayla especially liked to watch butterflies flit between the brightly colored flowers and bushes.

Today, though, as Makayla opened Eileen's backyard gate, there was something different. It was large and round with a big needle sticking up in the middle.

Eileen came out of the house just as Makayla moved closer to the stone circle.

"What's that?" Makayla asked.

"It's a sundial," the older woman explained. "Now I won't need to guess what time it is when I'm outside."

Eileen explained that by watching the shadow made by the big needle, she could tell the time.

"So now it's almost 11 o'clock," said Makayla.

"Right," said Eileen.

"The sundial doesn't need batteries," said Makayla.

"Right again," said Eileen. "The sundial also tells me it's time for a glass of lemonade."

Makayla smiled. She liked having Eileen for a friend.

Dear God,

Thank You for time to spend with friends. My favorite time of day is____. I pray to You in Jesus' name. **Amen.**

Let's Talk

Why is a sundial a good type of clock to use outside? The Bible tells us that any time is a good time to pray. When do you most often pray to God?

Parent Connection

A parent is the primary voice in a child's life. Your values, behaviors, and relationship patterns strongly impact your child. "Secondary voices" are those of coaches, pastors, teachers, grandparents, and other adults who have a significant role in a child's life. Encouraging relationships between your child and these people adds richness and depth beyond what is available in the immediate family.

Bringing It Home

• Ephesians 6:4 reminds us that the Christian parent has the joy and responsibility to teach a child about Jesus.

• A child's faith walk is most meaningful when taken alongside a loving adult who models for him a confident faith and God-pleasing lifestyle.

Let's Remember

If we hope for what we do not see, we wait for it with patience.
Romans 8:25

Waiting to Grow

Sophia kicked a clump of dirt. Then she stomped around the garden. She was mad; the seeds she planted were just not growing!

She had helped her mom drop every little seed directly into the row of earth. Then she had carefully covered up the seeds and patted down the dirt. And every day, Sophia watered the seeds from the heavy sprinkling can. Where were her flowers?

"It takes time for plants to grow," said her mom, kneeling alongside the muddy patch. "It might be another week before we see anything. Just think, Sophia, it's taken years for *you* to grow so tall."

"Humpf!" said Sophia as she stomped away. "Those flowers should grow right now!"

Let's Talk

If Sophia counted the days until the flowers grew, how long would she have counted? When you count the days until something happens, it is called a "countdown" because every day, you count fewer days. Have you ever done a birthday or holiday countdown?

Dear God,

It is so hard to wait, especially when
_____. Help me learn to be patient.
In Jesus' name. Amen.

Parent Connection

Children live in the "now." It takes years to understand abstract concepts like time and space, so it is hard for them to realize their birthday is still a month away. Whenever possible, link waiting time with a concrete idea that your child can see or hear. For example, you might say, "We'll go to Sunday School three more times before your birthday." Then they can physically mark off those dates on a calendar.

Bringing It Home

- We never have to wait to pray: God listens 24/7.

- Because Jesus loves us and forgives us, we are always blessed, all the time.

Playing Fair

"Seventeen, 18, 19, 20. Ready or not, here I come!" called Aaron. He ran straight toward the long row of shrubs. He had seen Kyle duck down behind the last bush.

"I found you!" Aaron said, looking down at the boy crouching behind the branches.

"That isn't fair!" said Kyle. "You cheated! I saw!"

"Yeah," said Peyton, coming out from behind the garage. "You're supposed to keep your eyes covered. But you peeked!"

"Let's do something else," said Kyle.

"I don't want to play with a cheater," said Peyton.

Dear God,

You know everything. Help me know how to be honest. I pray to You in Jesus' name. Amen.

Let's Talk

A person who cheats doesn't follow the rules. Have you ever played with a cheater? What happened?

Let's Remember

Call to Me and I will answer you.
Jeremiah 33:3

Who Will Be My Friend?

A tear dribbled down Ethan's cheek. Ethan's friend had moved to a new house, and Ethan wouldn't see his friend anymore. They couldn't dig in the backyard mud together. They wouldn't ride bikes down the street. Another tear dripped down Ethan's cheek.

"Who will be my friend?" Ethan asked his mom.

"Who do you know who likes to play with trucks?" asked his mom.

"John," said Ethan. "He has a tanker that is shiny and a cement mixer with a drum that really turns around."

"Tell me about John," his mom said.

"One time, he let me pour sand into the mixer," said Ethan. "We made a highway."

"Then let's see if John can play now," said his mom. "And Ethan, it was good that you told me you were feeling sad. If you feel sad again, you can come to me, and you can talk to God too. Both of us will always listen."

Let's Talk

Why was Ethan sad? What would make Ethan happy again? What makes someone a good friend?

Dear God,

I know I can always tell You how I feel. If I am sad or mad or happy or excited, You will listen to me. Thank You, God. In Jesus' name. Amen.

Parent Connection

A child might use the word *sad* to cover a wide range of feelings, including disappointment, unhappiness, loneliness, and frustration. Help your child build emotional literacy by using very specific words to identify your feelings. When a child hears you are angry, irritated, resentful, or furious, he begins to understand the shades of meaning that match the emotions.

Bringing It Home

- It is appropriate to cry when we lose a friend, as Jesus did when His friend Lazarus died.

- As Christians, we are confident we will be reunited with friends and loved ones in heaven, because Jesus has promised us eternal life.

Let's Remember

Good sense makes one slow
to anger. Proverbs 19:11

Madder Than Mad

Aiden was mad. He was furious.

He put on his meanest, maddest face. Then, folding his arms across his chest, he stomped away.

"I don't want a haircut!" he yelled. "I'm staying home!"

He stomped hard on every stair as he went up to his room. *Bam!* The house shook as he slammed the bedroom door.

A few minutes went by. Aiden kicked the bed, but then his foot hurt. He opened his closet to find something to play with, but he didn't find anything he liked. Not his robot, or the astronauts, or the new fire station.

His bedroom door opened.

"I see you're upset," his mom said as she walked into the room. "It's good that you are calming down. I can help. Let's both count to 10. One, two, . . ."

"I don't *want* to count," mumbled Aiden. "Don't *want* to settle down! Don't want a haircut!"

"Sometimes we have to do things we don't want to do," said his mom. "I really didn't want to get that flat tire fixed yesterday, but I had to do it anyway."

His mom stood.

"We're leaving in five minutes," she said. "Would you like a hug now or when you come downstairs?"

What do you think Aiden said?

Let's Talk

What helps you calm down when you are angry? In the Bible, God invites us to talk to Him about all our feelings, even when we are really, really upset. Do you ever do that?

Parent Connection

Help a child learn to cope with intense emotions by encouraging him to settle down in a safe, quiet place. This allows him to step back from his feelings. Or invite him to kick a soccer ball or squeeze play dough to physically work through his feelings. Counting to 10 and breathing deeply are coping mechanisms he can practice at home and use in public places.

Bringing It Home

- Prayer can defuse our anger. Although we might be frightened by the intensity of our anger, God isn't.

- When we repent of our sin, we enjoy the full benefits of forgiveness through Jesus.

Puppy in School

Dominic knelt next to the puppy. Over his furry gold coat, the puppy wore a red vest that read, "Service Dog in Training."

"Can I pet him?" Dominic asked the woman.

"Yes," said the lady. "His name is Brandy. Let him sniff your hand first. He's learning how to behave around children."

The puppy's wet nose tickled Dominic's fingers. Then Dominic reached to scratch under the dog's chin. Dominic asked, "Why is he wearing that vest?"

"His vest tells people that Brandy will be a guide dog some-day," said the lady. "I'm his puppy trainer. Brandy is living with me. He'll go everywhere I go until he starts school next year."

The puppy wagged his tail. Then he licked Dominic's hand.

"He likes me," said Dominic.

"And you're petting him very gently," said the lady. "At school, Brandy will learn to listen for danger and stop at curbs and stairs. Then he will be a partner for a person who needs help getting around."

Dominic continued to pet Brandy for a very long time. Finally, the puppy put his head on his paws and fell fast asleep.

Dear God,

Thank You for trainers who spend time teaching puppies how to behave. Thank You for dogs who help people. I think dogs are _____. In Jesus' name.
Amen.

Let's Talk

A blind person cannot see. How could you tell if someone is blind? How would you describe a dog to a blind person who had never seen a dog?

Parent Connection

Childhood is characterized by innocent curiosity. Children are born without prejudices. Their thoughts and feelings are gradually shaped by their experiences and observations of how others respond. Children learn to respect differences and accept diversity by healthy exposure to experiences and situations and by imitating our behavior.

Bringing It Home

- Asking faith-related questions is not a sign of spiritual weakness or lack of trust in God, but reflects a genuine desire to learn more about Him and the forgiveness we have through Jesus.

- The Holy Spirit encourages us to continually grow through God's Word.

A Real Princess

"That's my very favorite story," sighed Alexis, as her father closed the Bible. "I love how the princess found baby Moses in the basket and then adopted him."

"Do you think that's your favorite Bible story because we adopted you?" her dad asked.

"Maybe," said Alexis. "But I also like that a princess found baby Moses. You know I love *everything* about princesses."

"I know," smiled her dad as he glanced around the bedroom. The bed sheets, blankets, rug, and curtains all featured princesses wearing beautiful gowns. A princess doll, dressed in a satiny pink gown, sat on a pink pony. Alexis even had her very own tiara that sparkled on the dresser.

"Tomorrow night we can read a Bible story about a queen," said her dad.

"A real queen?" Alexis asked.

"A very brave real queen," said her dad. "But that's tomorrow night. Now, it's time for my favorite princess to close her eyes and go to sleep."

Dear God,

Thank You for giving us the Bible, which teaches about You and Jesus. In Jesus' name. Amen.

Let's Talk

In this story, Alexis was adopted. What does that mean? What is your favorite Bible story? Why do you like that story?

Parent Connection

After reading a story, children often ask, "Did that really happen?" Young children ask that question as they begin to differentiate between what's real and what's pretend. Older children ask the same question to learn more details and to verify their understanding that "Yes, that really happened."
To emphasize the facts of Scripture, some Bible scholars substitute the word *lesson* for *story* when referring to an episode in the Bible.

Bringing It Home

• In Baptism, God adopts us into His family.

• As members of God's family, we have millions of brothers and sisters who also believe in Jesus Christ as their Savior.

Honey in the Tummy

Savannah and Allison had played together all morning. Now the girls were hungry. Savannah's mom promised to help them make peanut-butter-and-honey wraps for lunch. They were Savannah's favorite, but Allison had never eaten them.

"It's easy," explained Savannah. "First you spread peanut butter on a tortilla."

Allison laid the round, thin tortilla on the plate. Then she slathered on peanut butter, being careful not to poke a hole in the tortilla.

"Now you pour on some honey," said Savannah. The girls both watched as honey dripped slowly out of the bottle, first on Savannah's tortilla, then on Allison's.

"Now you roll it up," instructed Savannah. Both

girls rolled up the tortillas. After praying, the girls bit off the ends of their tortillas. Savannah watched to see her friend's reaction.

"I like it," said Allison, licking stickiness off her fingers. "This is really good."

Savannah giggled and sang, "Yummy, yummy, yummy, I've got honey in my tummy."

Let's Talk

People in Bible times ate honey, just as we do. God even sent a special honey bread, called "manna," to Moses' people in the desert (Exodus 16:33). What ingredients did the girls in the story need to make their honey wraps? Why do you like honey?

Parent Connection

The many varieties of breadstuffs available today make it easy to expose a child to bread in many forms. From yeast breads, in round or rectangular loaves, and flatbreads, like pitas and tortillas, to bagels, which are boiled or steamed, a variety of breads can add an interesting element to a child's lunch box and discourage picky eating habits.

Bringing It Home

- Growing in the knowledge of Jesus, our Savior, is a healthy habit.

- We will be blessed when we are hungry to study God's Word.

Let's Remember

It is You [Lord] who have made the heavens and the earth by Your great power. Jeremiah 32:17

Let's Create!

Julian pounded the dough on the table. *Splat!* He was making very, very flat pancakes.

Julian pounded so hard that Destiny felt the table shake.

Destiny said, "I'm making a snake. *Sssss,*" she said, guiding a long snake toward him.

"Guess what I'm going to make now," Julian said. He scraped the flat pancakes off the table and rolled them into a ball. Holding the ball for Destiny to see, he asked, "What is it?"

"A ball?" she guessed.

"Nope," he said.

"An egg?" Destiny guessed. Julian stared at the round dough in his hand and shook his head.

"Well, what is it?" Destiny asked.

"The world," said Julian. "I am God. I made the world."

Let's Talk

Julian was pretending to be God. Long ago, when God created the world, He made a perfect place called the Garden of Eden. What animals would have lived in a perfect place like that? What sounds would you have heard in the garden?

Parent Connection

Educators encourage children to create with any type of modeling clay or dough because the results of this open-ended activity are limited only by a child's creativity. These activities have no right or wrong, and they often reflect a child's real-time experiences, areas of interest, and exposure to books and stories. As shown in this story, children who participate in open-ended activities approach the task from different perspectives and produce different results.

Bringing It Home

• We are the "crowning achievement" in God's creation.

• As disciples of the risen Savior, we respectfully manage and care for our world.

Let's Remember

Even the hairs of your head are
numbered. Luke 12:7

Fourteen Hairs

Alyssa counted: ". . . 10, 11, 12, 13, 14. That's all you have, Grandpa," she said, rubbing his shiny head. "You have 14 pieces of hair. I didn't count the fuzz."

"Well, that's just fine, Alyssa," he laughed. "Fuzz doesn't really count."

"Do you think you'll lose those hairs too?" Alyssa asked. "Then you'll be *really* bald."

Grandpa chuckled. "Most people would say I'm already bald," he said.

"The next time you come for a visit, I'll count again and see if you still have 14 hairs," she said.

"And now, should I count your hair?" Grandpa asked.

"Oh, no," said Alyssa. "We don't need to do that. I have hundreds or thousands or millions of hairs."

"You know, even before you started counting, Someone already knew I had fuzz and 14 hairs," Grandpa said. "Someone knows how many hairs you have too. Do you know who that is?"

Alyssa thought for a moment. She was sure she knew the answer, and she did.

"God," she said. "He knows everything."

Dear God,

You know so much about me. You know I like _____. And You know I love You. I pray to You in Jesus' name. Amen.

Let's Talk

Why was Alyssa counting the hairs on her grandpa's head? Who do you know who is bald? Who knows how many hairs are on your head?

Parent Connection

Young children idolize their parents. To them, we are heroes. When they discover we are merely heroes with feet of clay, some children get angry. They might be frustrated when we can't find their lost toy or buy them something they want. As we make mistakes and disappoint them, children gradually learn that not even their parents are perfect. That's a fact we need to remember too.

Bringing It Home

- As our Creator, God knows us better than anyone else.

- Jesus is aware of every one of our sins; He knows we continually need His forgiveness.

Let's Remember

He [the Lord] provides food.
Psalm 111:5

The Soup Chase

Anthony stirred his soup. He frowned. All kinds of things were floating in his bowl. He didn't like those floaters.

"Why did you put all those things in the soup?" Anthony asked his dad.

"Because they are good for you," his dad said.

"But they taste mushy," Anthony said. He dug deep in the bowl, then watched as little things plopped off his spoon.

"You like corn on the cob," said his dad. "That yellow thing is a kernel of corn. And you have great fun popping peas out of a pod. That little green ball is a pea."

Anthony wasn't convinced. He used his spoon to chase the veggies around the bowl. He caught a whole spoonful.

And then . . .

What do you think Anthony did next?

Dear God,

Thank You for food that tastes good. I especially like _____. In Jesus' name. **Amen.**

Let's Talk

Anthony found corn and peas in his soup. What do you sometimes find in your soup? Why is soup usually a healthy food?

Parent Connection

Sneaking healthy ingredients into foods can be a successful strategy for adding nutrients to a child's diet. But sometimes, serving food unmasked is just as effective. Although we commonly think of using dips or spreads with veggies, using fruit, whole wheat crackers, or multigrain bread can also be successful. Children often eat more when they are actively involved in the preparation process.

Bringing It Home

• When we are spiritually lost, Jesus, our Good Shepherd, finds us.

• Sometimes we discover God's blessings in unexpected places.

Moon Bath

"Bath time," called Dad.

Samantha pretended she didn't hear him. Instead, she continued to play with her new doll.

"Bath time, Sammy," he called again. "I've got the towel. You bring the pajamas."

Samantha decided to change her doll's clothes.

Dad appeared at Samantha's bedroom door. "Sammy, I know you like your new doll, but it's bath time," said Dad.

"I'm not dirty," Samantha said.

Her dad knelt beside her.

"I'll tell you what," he said. "You can have a moon bath."

"What's a moon bath?" asked Samantha.

"Bring some pajamas, then come and see," said her dad.

Samantha pulled out some pajamas and headed down the hall. Except for a little bit of light coming from under the bathroom door, everything was dark.

"Daddy?" she called. She did not like to be alone in the dark.

"In here," he said. Samantha pushed open the bathroom door. All the lights were off, except for a large flashlight shining toward the tub that was filling with water.

"A moon bath!" Samantha said.

Dear God,

Thank You for people who make things such fun, like _____. Thank You, God, for Jesus. Amen.

Let's Talk

Why did Samantha change her mind about taking a bath? Would it be hard to get clean in a moon bath? Is "moon bath" a good way to describe Samantha's bath?

Parent Connection

Adding creative touches can make everyday routines more fun for you and for your child. You might have a "backward day," when you serve hamburgers for breakfast and waffles for supper. Or, instead of reading this book when your child is tucked in bed, lay a blanket on the floor and read together on the story-time blanket or under an umbrella.

Bringing It Home

- Because God's timeline is not our timeline, we need to learn patience; we don't know everything He has planned for us.

- When things don't seem fair, we can remember that we have not earned our way to heaven—only Jesus' grace saves us.

Let's Remember

Whatever you do, work heartily,
as for the Lord. Colossians 3:23

A Smart Trade?

"I don't want to clean up," Ashley told her mom.

Ashley's play area was a mess. A stack of games had toppled over on the desk. Books were stacked on the floor, and it looked like someone had been searching through an entire open drawer for clothes.

"Let's make a bargain," said her mom. "You unpack and put away the groceries while I clean up in here."

Ashley thought about that. Emptying bags of groceries sounded better than cleaning up the messy room.

"Great," said Ashley as she dropped her doll on the floor and headed to the kitchen.

Full bags of groceries filled the room! One by one, Ashley emptied the bags. She stacked the cans in the cabinets. Then she used a stool to reach the cereal shelf. She carried the eggs carefully to the refrigerator. Her hands got cold putting away the ice cream and frozen vegetables. Ashley walked back and forth to the pantry and the cabinets and the grocery bags. She was working so hard!

Do you think Ashley was happy with her decision to trade jobs?

Dear God,

Thank You, God, for the people You send to help me. Thank You for the people who tell me about Jesus, like _____. In His name. Amen.

Let's Talk

Who does the grocery shopping at your house? Who puts away the groceries? The Bible says that when we help others, we can think of our work as serving God. What is one way you help around the house?

Parent Connection

In a healthy family, everyone contributes to the common good. That means even young children have jobs that help others. As a child grows up, her chores should change too, so that she gradually learns all the skills she will need when she lives independently. What life skill will you help your child practice today?

Bringing It Home

- We have many reasons to be thankful, but we are most grateful that Jesus is our Savior.
- Jesus uses the work we do to help others.

Let's Remember

I remember You upon my bed and
meditate on You in the watches of
the night. Psalm 63:6

Flashlight Tag

Christian continued to count: ". . . 44, 45, 46, 47, 48, 49, 50!"
Then he flicked on the flashlight in his hand and called, "Ready
or not, here I come!"

A shadow slinked between the trees. Clutching the light, he
raced toward the place where the shadow had appeared. No one
was there.

Creeping, he walked very slowly beside the garage.

After hearing a rustle in the leaves behind him, Christian
did not move. He held the flashlight still. Then he suddenly
turned around, and the light shined on Cameron.

"Gotcha!" said Christian.

Laughing, Cameron reached for the flashlight. "My turn," he
said, and started counting.

Let's Talk

The boys were playing a special kind of tag. What did they
need to play this game? Can you think of a reason someone
might not like this game?

Dear God,

Sometimes when it is dark outside, I feel _____. Help me remember that You are always with me, in the daytime and in the night. Through Jesus Christ alone. Amen.

Parent Connection

Being afraid of the dark is a common childhood fear. That is why some children sleep with a night-light or use a dimmer switch on bedroom lights. The lighted tank of an aquarium is ideal for older children: they are comforted by seeing the fish swim around and are not ridiculed for needing a night-light that can be too "babyish."

Bringing It Home

- The Bible shows us how people long ago turned to God when they were afraid, modeling behavior we can adapt today.

- We can be assured that no matter what happens, Jesus has secured eternal life for us.

Let's Remember

Whoever is slow to anger has great
understanding. Proverbs 14:29

Is Mad Bad?

Anna and her grandpa had enjoyed a wonderful day on the beach. They scrambled to stay dry as waves raced up the sand. They laughed as crabs scurried away. Grandpa helped pound sand into molds for Anna's castle. But now, dark clouds were building over the ocean. Grandpa said they had to leave before the storm came. He asked Anna to hurry and pack up.

Anna plopped down on the sand. She wasn't going to help. She was angry. "I don't want to go!" she said. Then Anna raced down the beach, making the sand fly. Anna yelled again and again, "I don't want to go!"

Grandpa folded their chairs and packed the sand buckets, watching as the dark clouds came closer. Grandpa reached for Anna's kite, but before he could tuck it into their bag, a wind gust pushed it away. The kite skittered down the beach.

Then Anna watched sadly as the wind carried the kite off above the waves. Then it crashed into the foaming water. "My kite, my kite!" she called as the colorful ribbons disappeared beneath the crashing waves.

Anna started to feel stinging rain and sand hit her face.

"Let's go, Anna," called her grandfather as he trudged to the car, overloaded with their beach gear. "Your kite is gone. It's starting to rain."

Tears streamed down Anna's cheeks as she struggled to stay upright in the wind.

What do you think happened next?

Let's Talk

When Anna got mad, she yelled and threw a fit. What do you do when you get mad?

Parent Connection

Being mad isn't bad. The problems come when a child doesn't know what to do with anger. Take every opportunity to model and teach coping techniques. Perhaps you count to 10—or 100—when you are angry. Even young children can learn to do that. Perhaps you work through your emotions at the gym. Children can express their anger by kicking a ball in the backyard or pounding play dough. When your child knows multiple coping strategies, she handles the emotion more effectively.

Bringing It Home

- We might get angry at God, but God will never stop loving us.

- Jesus died on the cross, even for people who are angry with Him.

Herbie

Herbie died today—but he wasn't the first one. Several weeks ago, the big goldfish died. Aubrey and her dad dug a hole next to the pink flower bush and buried the big fish.

Then, a few days later, the little goldfish died. Aubrey and her dad dug another hole next to the bush and buried the little fish.

And now, Herbie, the snail, had died.

Aubrey and her dad headed to the backyard to bury Herbie.

"Maybe Herbie isn't really dead," said Aubrey.

"Herbie hasn't moved for several days," said her dad. "He's really dead."

"Why do my pets keep dying?" asked Aubrey.

Her dad stopped digging and said, "I don't know if something in the water made them sick, or if it was just time for them to die."

Dear God,

Thank You for listening when I talk to You. I pray to You in Jesus' name. Amen.

Aubrey thought of how she had cared for her pets. She fed them. She changed the water in their bowl. She hung pictures of her pets on the refrigerator. Aubrey talked with her pets.

"I feel sad. Who will I talk to now?" asked Aubrey.

Her dad smiled.

"I'm here, and so is God," he said. "You can always talk to us."

Let's Talk

How did Aubrey feel? With whom do you talk when you are sad? Do you think Aubrey will get another pet?

Parent Connection

Often, a child's first experience with death is when a pet dies. Younger children don't understand that death is final, so they might ask when the animal will wake up. Although it might seem easier to hide a pet's death (such as flushing a fish down the toilet), be honest with your child. When comforting a child, avoid comments that link death with sleep. Assure your child that he did not cause the death. Remind the child that you and the rest of the family are nearby to be with him. Help your child focus on good times he enjoyed with his pet by looking at photos or videos.

Bringing It Home

- Jesus changes death from an end to the beginning of new life.
- Jesus died on the cross so that we do not die eternally.

Pop the Balloon!

Today was Ava's birthday, but she kept getting into trouble.

First she spilled the breakfast cereal. Then Ava tipped over her glass of juice. After that, she raced through the house. She was so eager to look at her presents again that she ran into her little brother and knocked him down.

"Ava, please settle down," said her mom.

"I can't," Ava said. "Today is not a sit-down day. Today is my BIRTHDAY!"

"Then let's go outside and use up some of that energy," said her mom. Using a piece of chalk, she drew a birthday cake on the driveway. Then she drew a candle and a present on the sidewalk.

"Now you draw a birthday picture over there," said her mom.

At the very end of the driveway, Ava drew a balloon. She colored it pink.

"Now, you and your brother can have a birthday race," Ava's mom said. "Who can be the first to reach the balloon?"

Ava and her brother raced toward the balloon.

"Pop!" said Ava, jumping up and down on the pink cement circle. "I'm popping the balloon because today is my birthday!"

Dear God,

Sometimes I get so excited that I don't know what to do. Thank You for special days, like _____.
In Jesus' name. Amen.

Let's Talk

Why did Ava keep getting into trouble? What is the most exciting day of the year for you? What makes that day so special?

Parent Connection

The days before birthdays and holidays are often stressful. Some of that tension is triggered by children who haven't learned how to contain or channel their excitement. Keep a list of infrequent chores that can occupy children before special days, like washing wastepaper cans or dusting living-room molding. These child-friendly jobs use up excess energy and fill time constructively.

Bringing It Home

- Every day is special when we recognize how Jesus works in our lives.

- We glorify God by helping others.

45

Let's Remember

Give thanks to the LORD, for He is good.
Psalm 136:1

Fun Choices

Brody had a huge grin on his face. Everywhere he looked, something exciting was happening. Old-fashioned cars were traveling along a narrow lane. He sniffed; he could definitely smell farm animals. Brody heard riders squeal as a parachute billowed down. This was his first time at the county fair, and he didn't know where to look next.

"Let's look at the map and decide where we want to go," said his mom.

"I want to ride a pony!" said Brianna, jumping up and down. Brody wasn't surprised; his sister played with her toy ponies all the time.

"You could ride a roller coaster, carousel, or even a real elephant," said their mom, looking at the big map.

"A real elephant?" asked Brody.

"Yes, and there are a lot of other great things to do too,"

Parent Connection

Choice mentality is a 21st-century value that's obvious when facing the yogurt section at the grocery store or cruising online shopping sites. Like us, children can feel overwhelmed when faced with multiple options. Help your child practice decision making by narrowing the options. Then encourage him to stick with his choice.

their mom said. "There's a magic show in 10 minutes. This afternoon, we can go to the puppet theater. You can climb a lookout tower. And there's a big model train display too."

"A pony ride, a pony ride!" repeated Brianna. "I want to ride a pony!"

"Okay, Brianna. Since you know what you want to do, let's start with your pony ride," said their mom. "Then, Brody, you can pick the next thing to do."

Brody started to feel nervous. He wanted to do everything, but how could he decide? What if he picked something that wasn't fun?

Bringing It Home

- God chooses us as His children because He loves us.
- Through the Bible, God has chosen to reveal the plan of salvation.

Let's Talk

What were some of the activities Brody could do at the fair? Why was Brody uncertain about what to choose?

A Kind Giant?

"Aaargh! Aaargh! I am a giant! Aaargh!"

Blake's aunt and uncle stopped talking. His mom stopped talking, and so did Blake's grandma.

"Aaargh! Aaargh!"

Everyone stared at Blake, who stomped around the room, taking giant steps.

Finally his mom asked, "Why are you a giant?"

"Because I knock down trees and houses!" he shouted, flinging his arms.

"Why do you do bad things?" his uncle asked.

"Because I'm a giant!" Blake said. "Aaargh!"

His mother stood up and walked to the kitchen. Blake still stomped around, taking one big step after another.

"It's too bad you're a giant," said his mom, coming into the room, holding a covered plate. "Uncle Art brought some of his super special brownies that are only for people who are nice and kind."

"Oh, that's me!" said Blake, reaching to take off the plate cover. "I'm nice and kind."

Do you think Blake got to eat a brownie? Why?

Dear God,

I try to be kind to others. I am kind when I _____. Help me to always remember to be kind like Jesus was. In His name. Amen.

Let's Talk

In the Bible, we read about the giant named Goliath who was very tall (1 Samuel 17:4). Goliath was not a kind giant. The tallest giant in the Bible was a king named Og. Even his bed was big (Deuteronomy 3:11). Can a tall person be as kind as a short person?

Parent Connection

A child begins to understand kindness after experiencing and seeing examples. We might tell a child, "Be kind to your sister." However, by adding a few additional words, we help him understand the meaning of kindness—for instance, "Be kind to your sister. Help her pour the juice." Identify situations throughout the day that offer opportunities to define the virtue through actions.

Bringing It Home

• Jesus showed God's kindness to everyone when He gave Himself for our sins.

• Those who follow Jesus' example will be kind to others without expecting a reward.

Let's Play!

"Now I'm going to shampoo your hair," said Abigail. "Keep your eyes closed so the soap doesn't sting."

Abigail carefully soaped her doll's scalp before dumping cup after cup of water over her head. Soap bubbled right up Abigail's arms.

"What are you doing?" asked her brother, Andrew.

"I'm giving my doll a bath and shampoo," she said.

"That's silly girl stuff," frowned Andrew.

"That's okay," said Abigail. Turning to the doll, she said, "We like girl stuff, don't we?"

Andrew continued to watch as Abigail soaped and rinsed her doll again and again before wrapping her carefully in a small towel.

As Abigail pulled the sink stopper to let out the soapy water, she said, "You play with dolls too."

"Do not," said Andrew. "I play with *action figures*."

Let's Talk

In what ways are action figures and dolls similar? What is one way you take care of your toys?

Parent Connection

Gender differences become apparent in early childhood. Research shows that girls choose toys that allow them to nurture and build relationships. In general, boy toys involve action, motion, and competition. Some of those early preferences are still evident when school-age children play video games. In what ways are these themes reflected in your child's play?

Bringing It Home

• To think, say, or do anything against God counts as a sin.

• God does not count our sins; through Jesus, He forgives them.

Let's Remember

Go into all the world and proclaim
the gospel to the whole creation.
Mark 16:15

A Grumpy Angel

Brandon frowned as his mom carefully draped the angel costume over her arm. The halo almost got tangled in the flowing sleeves.

"We need to be careful," she said, lifting the costume even higher.

Brandon felt like kicking dirt on the white robe. He wanted to rip apart the golden halo. In the church play, he was supposed to wear a robe that looked like a dress!

"Too girly," he grumbled again and again as they walked into the building. "I wanted to be a shepherd."

A boy waved excitedly. "Hey, Brandon!" he called. "Got your halo?"

"It's too girly," said Brandon.

His friend was puzzled. He looked down at the glittery halo in his hand. "Angels are God's messengers," he said. He liked dressing as God's helper. "Come on. We've got to get ready."

Let's Talk

Angels are God's messengers; we are too. What message do you share about Jesus?

Parent Connection

Acting out Bible stories gives children an opportunity to physically support, enrich, and integrate their cognitive learning. Old Testament lessons that are especially easy to act out, with or without costumes or props, include the Seven Days of Creation (Genesis 1–2), Noah's Ark (Genesis 6–8), the Tower of Babel (Genesis 11:1–9), Baby Moses (Exodus 2:1–10), the Walls of Jericho (Joshua 5:13–6:20), and David and Goliath (1 Samuel 17:1–52).

Bringing It Home

- God created the angels to serve as His messengers and guardians.

- God created us to do a very special job for Him: to tell others about Jesus and His Gospel message.

Let's Remember
Then I saw a new heaven and a
new earth. Revelation 21:1

A Heavenly View

Brooke and her mom were both breathing hard. They had climbed the high hill in the center of the park.

"Let's stop here," panted her mom, collapsing on the grass. Brooke sat down and stretched out. Looking up at the gray sky, she said, "I wonder if it's cloudy in heaven today."

"Well, we won't get mosquito bites in heaven," said her mom, slapping at a bug.

"And if I fall down, I won't skin my knee," said Brooke, checking the bandage on her leg.

Brooke and her mom were quiet, just thinking.

"In heaven, we'll always have enough money to buy a double-scoop ice-cream cone," said Brooke.

"Maybe ice-cream cones are free," said her mom, pushing to stand up. "We need to get going. It might not rain in heaven, but those are raindrops falling on my head right now."

Let's Talk

Why do you think Brooke and her mom were talking about heaven? What do you think heaven looks like? What will be the best thing about heaven?

Parent Connection

Heaven can seem far away when we are overwhelmed by the challenges of raising a happy, loving child. Yet the promise of heaven is very real. St. Paul writes that the joy we'll experience in heaven will last forever (2 Corinthians 4:18). Anticipating endless joy is especially uplifting during times of difficulty or sadness. Children may visualize heaven as a toy store or amusement park, but we can focus on Jesus' promises of salvation and the unlimited joy and peace He brings.

Bringing It Home

- The only way to reach heaven is by believing in Jesus as our Savior.

- Jesus gave up being in heaven so we could be saved from sin and eternal death.

Let's Remember

For those who love God all things
work together for good.
Romans 8:28

Changing Times

"Why the sad face?" asked Grandma.

"Mommy doesn't have time to read to me, again," said Adam. "She promised to read after she feeds the baby, but she's always too busy."

Grandma pulled Adam toward her.

"There's a place right here labeled 'Adam,'" said his grandmother, patting the sofa.

"Will *you* read to me?" Adam asked.

"I will, but I thought you might want to talk first," said his grandma.

"Not about the baby," said Adam.

"Not about the *new* baby, but a baby who came to this house a few years ago," she said.

"Me?" said Adam.

"Right. A little baby who cried at night and needed lots of new diapers and who everybody loved so much," said Grandma.

Adam wasn't sure he liked hearing about himself as a baby. He shoved the book toward her. "Please read," he said.

Dear God,

Sometimes it's hard to get used to new things. When things change, help me remember I can always talk to You about what's happening. In Jesus' name. **Amen.**

Let's Talk

Do you know a family with a new baby? What does the baby do? When you were a baby, what did you do that all babies do?

Parent Connection

Before a new baby arrives, it's important to talk with the big sister or big brother about what to expect. That is because sibling rivalry begins long before a second or third infant is born. Preparing for a new sibling triggers multiple changes. A child may respond by being aggressive or regressive. Immediately after the birth, a child realizes he has a new position in the family. Adjustments take time, but being especially alert to a child's physical and emotional needs will make the transition go more smoothly.

Bringing It Home

• Even when we feel unlovable, God always loves us.

• God's love never changes.

Let's Remember

I praise You, for I am fearfully
and wonderfully made.
Psalm 139:14

A Hairy Problem

Caleb watched as his mom tried to put a hat on his baby sister. Each time his mom tried to tie the hat, baby Sydney pulled it off. On and off. On and off. Caleb started to laugh. It became a game. On and off. On and off. Baby Sydney laughed too.

Their mother did not laugh.

"Caleb, you're not being helpful," said his mom. "Sydney needs to wear a hat."

"Why?" he asked.

"You have hair on your head," she said. "Your sister will get sunburned if her head isn't covered."

Sydney was almost completely bald.

Caleb thought for a moment. Then he said, "I have an idea."

He pushed the stroller off the sidewalk and headed toward a tree.

What was Caleb's idea?

Let's Talk

Why did Sydney pull off her hat? God gave us hair to keep our heads from getting sunburned. What else do you use to protect yourself from the sun?

Dear God,

Thank You for the shampoo I use to _____ my hair. Thank You for _____ that protects me from the sun. Thank You, in Jesus' name. Amen.

Parent Connection

A child is a blessing. That blessing multiplies as a family grows. The way a child learns to communicate, solve problems, and approach life is shaped by those closest to him. Although peers are among the strongest "outside influences" during later years, sibling relationships are primary during childhood. When siblings get together in later years as adults, they often slip into the same roles they had as children.

Bringing It Home

- God protects us because He is our loving heavenly Father.

- Jesus guards us against Satan.

Let's Remember

Let Your steadfast love comfort me.
Psalm 119:76

The Dollhouse

Avery loved playing with her friends at their houses. Each of the other girls had a dollhouse.

Trinity's dollhouse had a fancy room with mirrors and a piano. Her dollhouse family had a cat named Bella.

Jennifer's dollhouse had an elevator that went up and down and a doorbell that went *ding-dong*.

Emma had a pink house, and it looked like a palace for her princess doll. There was a curved staircase that went up to the bedroom, and a canopy hung high above the bed.

Avery didn't have a real dollhouse. She stacked together two cardboard boxes to make a house. She colored the inside of the boxes to make the walls look pretty, but Avery wanted a real dollhouse for her birthday.

On the night before her birthday, her mom hugged her tightly and said, "Honey, I know you want a dollhouse for your birthday, but we can't afford it right now. We've gotten you some nice clothes, though, so you'll have presents to open."

Even though her mom was hugging her, Avery felt sad.

Dear God,

Some children will be unhappy when they go to bed tonight. Please help them know that You are with them and love them very much. In Jesus' name. Amen.

Let's Talk

Why did Avery like to play at her friends' houses? How would you cheer up Avery?

Parent Connection

"Everybody has one" starts as a repetitive whine during the early school-age years. Because peers become increasingly important, a child naturally compares himself to others. To fit in, he thinks he needs what others have. That is not always possible; that's not even always a good thing. When a child asks for something that "everybody" has, you can say, "Tell me why you need it." Older children can begin to differentiate between needs and wants. They can also accept alternatives for purchasing desired items. For example, they might designate birthday money or do extra chores to earn money.

Bringing It Home

- The most unfair thing in the world was Jesus' death on the cross.

- It isn't fair that Jesus forgives us, but He does!

Let's Remember

He who dwells in the shelter of the Most High will abide in the shadow of the Almighty. Psalm 91:1

Shadow Play

"You can't catch me," sang Carson as he slipped around a corner.

"But I got your shadow," said Jordan, jumping on top of Carson's shadow. "Hey, let's play shadow tag! And you're 'it.'"

Carson darted out, eager to step on Jordan's shadow. The boys chased each other's shadows until both were out of breath.

"It's time for supper," said Carson. "See you tomorrow."

On the walk home, Jordan experimented with his shadow by twisting in different directions. When he danced down the sidewalk, his shadow went wild! During supper, Jordan looked out the window and watched as the shadow of the house grew on the lawn when the sun went down. And later, while waiting for his dad to tuck him into bed, he used his hands to make shadows of a dog and a bird on his bedroom wall.

"All set for prayers?" his dad asked.

"I'm making shadows," said Jordan. His dad watched as a shadowy snake slithered up the wall. As Jordan moved his hands away from the wall, the snake got larger. Up close, the snake looked like a worm.

Dear God,

Thank You for fun things to do all around the house. I especially like to _____. In Jesus' name. **Amen.**

"My turn," said his dad. "I'm going to make something that will tell you what time it is."

His dad used his fingers to make a cross.

Let's Talk

To make a shadow, you need a light and something to block the light. Where did Jordan find shadows? What time was it when Jordan's dad made a cross shadow? What shadows can you make?

Parent Connection

"Everyday science" could be the title of a school curriculum or the umbrella label for many of the concepts a child learns informally through everyday activities. Potential lessons are all around. When a child makes a ramp and zooms cars down it, you can say, "You just made a simple machine. That ramp is called an 'incline plane.'" When a child is aware of what to look for, he will identify the same simple machine when you drive a car down a parking garage ramp or when he rides a theme park roller coaster. Whenever possible, help your child connect academic concepts with everyday objects.

Bringing It Home

• The cross is God's "plus sign," showing that we are given life in heaven in addition to earthly life.

• The cross reminds us of Jesus' death and resurrection on our behalf.

Let's Remember

The LORD will give what is good,
and our land will yield its increase.
Psalm 85:12

On the Farm

Charles was excited to visit his aunt and uncle's farm. It had been dark when he arrived last night, so he was eager to see everything this morning. Through the bedroom window, Charles saw a red barn and some tractors. A tall silo cast a long shadow across the yard.

He could see his aunt carrying a basket out of a fenced yard where chickens were making a lot of noise. Charles wondered if they would eat eggs for breakfast.

From the other window, Charles watched his uncle leave the big red barn where the cows lived. Perhaps they would drink milk for breakfast. He raced down the stairs, eager to see what else was happening.

"Good morning, Charles," said his uncle, coming into the kitchen. "Did you sleep well?"

"Oh, yes," Charles said. "But I wanted to watch what happens on a farm in the morning."

"It's just like at your house," his uncle explained. "After doing chores, we eat breakfast. I'll start by rinsing the berries we picked yesterday."

Charles leaned against the counter and watched as his aunt set eggs on the table. His uncle took milk and berries from the refrigerator. Charles heard his stomach growling.

Dear God,

Thank You for farmers who work hard, caring for animals and riding tractors to raise good food for me to eat. In Jesus' name. **Amen.**

What do you think Charles ate for breakfast?

Let's Talk

What is your favorite breakfast? Although your family probably buys eggs and milk from a store, somewhere a farmer raised the chickens and cows that produced that food. How would your life be different if you lived on a farm?

Parent Connection

Did your child practice creative thinking when he answered these questions? Your child might have suggested that Charles ate scrambled eggs and drank a glass of milk for breakfast. But he might also have said blueberry pancakes or waffles. We can often stretch a child's creative thoughts. In this example, you might ask, "What could they make using milk, eggs, and berries?" Stay alert for opportunities to extend and expand your child's thinking skills.

Bringing It Home

• Disciples of Jesus will want to help those who are hungry.

• The most important meal we eat is the Lord's Supper, which reminds us that Jesus gave Himself for us so that we might have forgiveness of sins and life everlasting.

Let's Remember

Each will have to bear his own load.
Galatians 6:5

Oh, Dear

Chloe dragged her feet. She knew her mom would be upset.

"Come on in, Chloe," her mom said, opening the door. Warm air coming out of the house felt so good, especially on Chloe's cold head.

Her mom said, "I watched out the window, and it looked like you had fun in the snow."

Chloe took off one boot. Then she kicked off the other. Next, she took off her mittens.

"Your ears look red," said her mom. With her hands, she gently covered Chloe's ears.

"Oh, Chloe, your ears are freezing! Even your hair is cold. Where is your hat?" she asked.

Two big tears slipped down Chloe's red, cold face.

"I lost it," she sobbed. "I didn't mean to. I thought it got buried under the snow. I dug and dug, but I couldn't find it."

"Oh, Chloe," sighed her mom. "Things just keep losing you. First it was a jacket, then that school paper I was to sign, and now your hat."

"You aren't mad?" Chloe asked.

Dear God,

Help me admit when I make a mistake and keep my promise to do better. In Jesus' name. **Amen.**

"I'm disappointed," said her mom. "We talked about being responsible and taking better care of your things. What can we do about this?"

Let's Talk

Being responsible means that others can count on you. In this story, how could Chloe show she was responsible? In what ways do you show that you are dependable?

Parent Connection

Developing a sense of responsibility is a sign that your child is growing up. However, becoming a dependable person takes time and repeated opportunities to demonstrate that maturity. As you adjust a child's household duties to match his increasing abilities, do not merely add more tasks, but substitute jobs that require higher-level skills.

Bringing It Home

• As responsible people, we do what God asks.

• On the cross, Jesus took responsibility for the sins of the entire world.

Let's Remember

A new commandment I give to you, that you love one another: just as I have loved you, you also are to love one another.
John 13:34

A Loving Feeling

Christopher loved to pet his dog's fur. Spike liked it too. He wagged his tail, and every so often, he opened his sleepy eyes.

"You certainly like that animal," said his aunt.

"I can feel his love," said Christopher. "When I put my fingers deep in his fur, I can feel that Spike loves me."

"Can you feel my love when I give you a hug?" his aunt asked, reaching out to put her arms around Christopher.

He nodded.

"I can feel love all over this
room," said Christopher. "There's
love in this whole, big, entire house."

"God has given us a wonderful
family," agreed his aunt. "We're all a
part of God's family too. That makes
us special."

Let's Talk

Which family members live with
you? Which family members live in
other places?

Parent Connection

Some abstract concepts
are difficult for children
to understand, but love
is one of the easiest to
teach: there are simply so
many ways to demonstrate
love. Of course, when we
comfort a sick child in
the middle of the night or
make a special effort to
prepare a favorite food, a
child doesn't say, "Mommy
loves me." However, our
repeated, caring actions
communicate clearly with-
out words. Because God
surrounds us with His love,
a similar type of love flows
easily and consistently
from our parent-heart.

Bringing It Home

- God shows His love for
  us in many ways, most
  importantly by sending
  Jesus to be our Savior
  from sin.

- We can share Jesus' love
  because He first loved
  us.

Let's Remember

Be kind to one another.
Ephesians 4:32

Boo!

Jayden felt like being mischievous. He pulled a blanket off the bed. Then he put the blanket over his head. Covered completely, he peeked out through a tiny space. Walking ever so slowly, he tiptoed into his little brother's room.

"Boo!" said Jayden.

Baby Joseph looked up. He started to cry.

"Oh, Jayden," said their mom. "You've scared Joseph."

"Boo!" said Jayden again. Crying, baby Joseph reached for his mom.

"Joseph doesn't know you're under the blanket," she explained. "He thinks you are a ghost."

"Boo!" said Jayden.

"Come here, Jayden," said his mom, pulling him toward her. The blanket slipped off.

"Boo!" said Jayden. "It's me."

Joseph stopped crying and looked. Smiling through his tears, the baby reached toward his brother.

His mom smiled, holding her two boys close. Turning to Jayden, she asked, "Doesn't it feel better to see someone smile?"

Dear Jesus,

When someone is unkind, help me remember I can always tell You what happened. I feel safe when I talk with You. In Jesus' name. Amen.

Let's Talk

How did Jayden scare his little brother? Do you think Jayden was having fun? Has someone ever scared you?

Parent Connection

Acting like a bully is not a natural stage that a child goes through. Research shows that bullying can be learned very early in life. If your child appears to delight in making others uncomfortable, make an extra effort to model caring for others. Set and enforce consistent limits. Make sure your child understands that it is always better to be kind than to be mean. Repeatedly affirm your child with both words and a hug when you catch him being good.

Bringing It Home

- God's rules, the Law, protect us from ourselves and others.

- Jesus kept God's rules perfectly so His death could win our freedom from sin. That's the Good News of the Gospel.

Claire's Corner

"Claire? Are you upstairs?" her mother called.

Claire didn't answer, but Princess peered down from the top of the stairs, then silently padded down.

Looking at the kitty who was now meowing at her feet, Claire's mom said, "Well, you're not Claire. Do you know where she is?"

"Meow," said Princess as she stretched out on the carpet.

Claire's mom called for her daughter as she walked throughout the house. Finally, stepping outside, Claire's mom called even louder, "Claire?"

Branches brushed against the side of the house as Claire emerged from behind a large bush.

"What are you doing back there?" asked her mother.

"That's my secret corner," said Claire, pointing behind the bush. "Now it's not secret anymore."

"What do you do back there?" asked her mom, peering through the branches. She could see a row of Claire's jewelry lined up next to her jewelry box.

"Today I'm playing jewelry store," explained Claire, "but sometimes I just sit in my corner."

Dear God,

I know if I'm ever lonesome, I can talk to You. I can even tell You a secret. In Jesus' name. Amen.

Reaching for a hug, her mom whispered, "I'll keep Claire's Corner a secret."

"Promise you won't tell?" Claire asked.

"I promise," her mom smiled.

Let's Talk

Playing with friends is fun, but sometimes it's fun to be alone. What do you like to play when you are by yourself? Do you talk to God when you are alone or when you are with others?

Brave Boys

"You'll need to hold still," Grandpa said, holding the medicine and box of bandage strips.

"No," said David, limping away. "See? I can run with the splinter in my foot."

Grandpa shook his head. "We need to remove that splinter before it goes deeper into your foot," he said. "Come on now. Didn't we just read a story about a brave boy with the same name as yours?"

David limped slowly across the room. He climbed even more slowly onto a chair.

"Now hold still," said Grandpa, taking the injured foot in his hand. "Tell me that story of the brave David in the Bible."

"He fought a giant," mumbled David.

"Do you think that David was afraid?" Grandpa asked, turning David's foot toward the light.

"Maybe," mumbled David. "But God was with him."

"Can you ask God to be with you too?" Grandpa asked.

"Ouch!" said David. He squeezed his eyes tight. "That hurt."

Grandpa gently smoothed medicine over the place where the splinter had been. Then he said, "Now I know about *two* brave boys named David."

Let's Talk

A brave person faces a situation that is difficult or dangerous. The title of this story is "Brave Boys." Who were the brave boys? In the Bible, read the story about a brave boy who meets a giant (1 Samuel 17:32–40, 48–50).

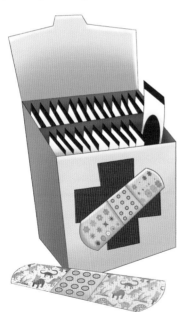

Parent Connection

Children naturally identify with the biblical David. After all, he was a brave young man. David modeled the fearlessness and the faith our children need to face problems in their lives. When reading Bible stories with your child, try to identify a single character trait to emphasize during the lesson. Then look for ways to highlight that trait in everyday situations.

Bringing It Home

- In the Bible, we read about David's courage, which came from trusting in God for protection.

- Jesus defeats the giant in our life—sin—by forgiving our sin and promising us salvation.

Let's Remember

I bless the LORD who gives me counsel.
Psalm 16:7

Mad Ben

Benjamin tossed his soccer shoes into the kitchen corner and stood with his arms crossed.

"What's the matter?" asked his mom.

"One of the kids at soccer practice said Benjamin was a lousy player," explained his dad.

"Well, dinner's almost ready," said his mom. "You will feel better when you eat."

But at dinner, Benjamin was still upset. He kicked his sister under the table. Then he teased his little brother and grabbed his fork.

"Benjamin," said his dad, "I'm sorry practice didn't go well, but you can't take out your feelings on your sister and brother. We'd like you to sit here and eat with us, but if you can't behave, then you can go to your room."

What do you think Benjamin did?

Dear God,

I can talk to You even when I'm mad. One time, I got mad when _____. I pray to You in Jesus' name. **Amen.**

Let's Talk

In the Bible, we read about a leader of God's people named Moses. One time, he got so mad, he threw the Ten Commandments, which God had written on a big stone. The stone broke apart (Exodus 32:19). When you're mad, what do you do?

Parent Connection

A child often redirects anger away from himself toward those who are closest to him. When an adult intervenes, that action is keenly watched by all the children, not just the child who is acting out. Tailor your approach to match your child. For example, sometimes a child responds to empathy, to understanding about what happened. Other times, a child responds to a ritual: take deep breaths and count to 10. Still other times, a child wants to tell what happened in his own words, so listen without judgment. A single strategy will rarely work all the time, so identify several approaches to use.

Bringing It Home

- God can defuse anger through a conversation with Him.

- Jesus died on the cross for all our sin.

Let's Remember
I was glad when they said to me,
"Let us go to the house of the LORD!"
Psalm 122:1

Is This a Church?

Diego held his grandpa's hand as they left the parking lot.

"Now remember, Diego," reminded his grandfather. "This church looks very different from yours. But we all worship the one true God."

Diego nodded. He could already see that the outside of the building was different. His church had a tall steeple. This church looked like his daddy's office building.

The front doors were wide open. Already, Diego could see the inside was different too. There was a big room with rows of chairs. Basketball nets hung from both ends of the room.

Protective wire crisscrossed windows high on the walls. A scoreboard hung at the very back. Bleachers were pushed against the wall. Grandpa went to church in a gym!

"This isn't a church," whispered Diego.

"This is a gym on most days," whispered Grandpa. "But on weekends, it is used as a church."

"But this doesn't have pretty windows or pews," said Diego.

"God is here, though," said Grandpa. "Sing along with us and listen as we read from the Bible. You'll see that a church can even meet in a gym."

Dear God,

Thank You for my church. I especially like _____. At church, I learn about Jesus, my Savior. In His name. **Amen.**

Let's Talk

Do you think Diego liked worshiping in his grandfather's church? What do you especially like about your church? How would you tell a friend what your church looks like?

Joys of Life

Chase loved to visit Mrs. Keller. She sometimes gave him cookies, but that wasn't the real reason he liked to go to her house. She always made him feel happy.

"Hi, Mrs. K," he called. "It's sunny today."

"I can feel that," said Mrs. Keller. She was almost blind, but she knew what the weather was by how light it was and by how the air felt. Today, she was sitting on the porch, where the sun was warming her arms.

"I brought you something," Chase said. "I'll put the plate on your table."

"I can smell your cookies," she said. "Did you help make them?"

Chase carefully placed the plate on the table. Then he perched on the top step next to her chair.

"I didn't stir in the chips this time, but I've been eating the cookies," said Chase. "What are you doing today?"

"Just enjoying being alive," she said. "God made a wonderful world and blessed me with a good friend."

For the rest of the afternoon, Chase and Mrs. Keller sat on the porch and talked.

Dear God,

Thank You for people who spend time with me, like _____. In Jesus' name. **Amen.**

Let's Talk

Why do you think Chase liked to visit his neighbor? Mrs. Keller said Chase was a "good friend." What makes a person a good friend?

Parent Connection

Children connect easily with people who express an interest in them. When visiting with a friend or relative who is unfamiliar to your child, ask your child to bring photos, schoolwork, or favorite items to trigger conversation. Because children like to talk about themselves and adults like to listen, everyone benefits.

Bringing It Home

- God wants us to respond to His love by showing that love to others. We do this when we care for them.

- Jesus showed us that He loves us when He came to earth and then gave His life on the cross for our sins.

The Web Spinner

Gavin and Dylan crouched in the corner. The boys were silent. So was the spider. The brothers watched as the spider crawled up and down, spinning around, creating more lines in the web. Back and forth, here and there, around and around it went.

"You're so quiet in here. What's going on?" Mom asked as she walked into the room.

"Shhh," whispered Dylan. "The spider is spinning a web."

The three of them watched as the spider continued to weave.

"That spider is making a net to catch supper," Mom quietly explained. "Perhaps it will catch a tasty bug. But you don't need to hunt for your supper. Food is on the table."

"Let's eat," said Gavin.

Let's Talk

Why is this story called "The Web Spinner"? Is this a good title? A spider uses a web to catch food. What food can get caught in a web?

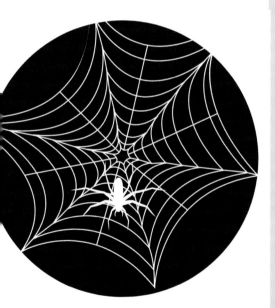

Parent Connection

A spiderweb, perhaps like the one that captured the boys' attention, is actually mentioned in the Bible. In Job (8:13–15), we read that those who don't trust God end up clinging to things as flimsy as a spider's web. Our world is filled with fears, known and unknown, but we hold on tight to God. Like a child who counts on us to catch him at the bottom of the slide, we are confident that God will keep His promises to us.

Bringing It Home

- God created everything and everyone for a purpose.

- God calls us to be faithful parents, which means our top priority is to share with our child the Good News of salvation in Christ Jesus.

Let's Remember

Be strong and let your heart take courage. Psalm 27:14

Real Courage

"Leg high. Lock ankle. Bend knee," Eli said as Brady kicked toward the net. "Good one. Now it's my turn."

"Leg high. Lock ankle. Bend knee," Brady reminded Eli as he took a shot.

The boys were practicing goal kicks just as their soccer coach had instructed. They wanted to be ready to play for their next game.

"Whoops!" said Brady. The ball sailed through the air, then rolled down the sidewalk. The ball kept rolling. Eli chased it. But he stopped when he saw someone else holding the ball.

"Looks like I have a new soccer ball," smirked a big kid.

Dear God,

Sometimes it's hard to be brave. Help me have courage to do the right thing. In Jesus' name. Amen.

"That's our ball," said Eli, panting after the long run.

"Let's fight for it," said the big kid. Dropping the ball behind him, he put up his fists. "Come on, chicken. Are you afraid to fight for your little ball?"

Eli wasn't sure what to do. He wanted to get the ball back, but his mom had taught him to walk away from trouble. And that's just what he did.

Let's Talk

Eli needed courage to walk away from that bully. Courage is doing what's right, even when it's hard. Do you know someone who has courage?

Parent Connection

Playground bullying has taken a dangerous turn. As we are reminded by headline news, harassment can become a life-or-death issue. Sadly, most children will experience some form of bullying, so teaching a child techniques to manage such situations has taken on a sense of urgency. "If there's trouble, walk away" is a solution that might require courage, but it is effective for children of all ages.

Bringing It Home

• Jesus showed ultimate courage when He went to the cross.

• Jesus did this to fulfill God's promise of a Savior; His sacrifice was a clear demonstration of His love for us.

Let's Remember
I have called you by name,
you are Mine. Isaiah 43:1

Honey

"Why do you call me 'Honey'?" Emily asked her aunt.

"Because you are as sweet as honey," she explained. "You helped your sister when she fell, and you offered to set the table for supper. You were kind and thoughtful—as sweet as honey."

"My friends call me 'Em.' That's short for 'Emily.' Mommy calls me 'Emily Elizabeth' when she's angry. You're the only one who calls me 'Honey,'" said Emily.

Her aunt was quiet for a moment.

"Is it all right that I call you 'Honey'?" she asked.

Then Emily was quiet for a moment as she thought about her aunt's question.

What do you think Emily said?

Dear God,

There are so many people in the world, but You know *my* name. That makes me feel _____. I pray to You in Jesus' name. Amen.

Let's Talk

People often have a first name, middle name, and last name. What is your whole name? Ask your mom or dad, "Why did you choose this name for me?"

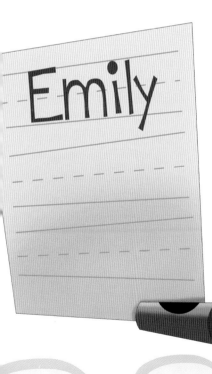

Parent Connection

A name is an important element of personal identity. At 4 months, a baby begins to recognize his own name. Between 8 and 12 months of age, he will respond when his name is said. When parents choose a name for their baby, they are taking an early step toward publicly claiming the baby as a family member.

Bringing It Home

- We share the name "Christian" with people throughout the world who also believe in Jesus as their Savior.

- The world population continues to grow, yet God not only knows who we are, but He even knows how many hairs are on our head.

Let's Remember

Bring two of every sort into the
ark to keep them alive with you.
Genesis 6:19

Tunnel Talk

Cole loved going to the zoo. He liked the monkeys that swung from branch to branch and the penguins that waddled. He especially liked driving a jeep in the children's zoo and playing in the tunnel.

"Tunnel's coming up," Cole said, running ahead of his parents. "Listen for me."

Soon, his parents heard a very loud voice say, "I like monkeys!" Then, "I like monkeys!" echoed again and again, a little quieter each time. His parents couldn't see Cole yet, but they knew exactly where he was.

Then, the same loud voice said, "I like penguins!" Then, "I like penguins!" echoed again and again through the tunnel.

Dear God,

Thank You for making so many great animals. The funniest animal in the zoo is _____. In Jesus' name.
Amen.

When Cole's parents reached the tunnel, they asked, "What are you going to announce next?"

Cole thought for a moment, then said, "God made animals!" Again, the voice echoed the message. But as the echo grew softer, it was replaced by a loud voice saying, "God made you too!"

Cole smiled and his parents chuckled. Someone else had heard Cole's message!

Let's Talk

What did Cole like about the zoo? Many years ago, God told a man named Noah to put two of every animal on a very big boat called an ark. Some of those animals are the same kind that live in zoos today. How many animals can you name?

Let's Remember

A joyful heart is good medicine.
Proverbs 17:22

The Banana Joke

Eric asked, "What did the baby banana say to his mom?"

Eric's mom said, "I have no idea."

"Oh, Mom, that's not the answer. The banana said, 'I don't *peel* good'—get it?" said Eric, laughing because *peel* rhymes with *feel.*

"Where do you hear these silly jokes?" asked his mom.

"Cooper tells them to me," said Eric.

"I'm trying to get supper ready," his mom said. "If you have more jokes, go tell your sister."

Eric knocked on his sister's door. She always closed the door when she did homework. Eric opened her door and said, "Paige, what did the baby banana say to his mom?"

Paige looked up from the computer and said, "Eric, I'm working, and I have no idea about your silly joke."

"'I don't *peel* good,'" said Eric, laughing again at the silly answer.

Paige didn't even smile as she gently shooed him out the door.

Why won't anyone laugh with me? Eric wondered.

Dear God,

Everybody can smile when they think about You, because You're wonderful. Thank You for sending Jesus as my Savior. In His name. **Amen.**

Let's Talk

Eric interrupted his mom and sister, who were busy. If Eric told a joke when his family was sitting together at supper, do you think they would laugh? Are all jokes funny?

Parent Connection

Making time to laugh at a child's silly jokes may seem like an unimportant task during a busy day. And yet, "found moments," those 30-second spaces between tasks, offer an opportunity to listen to a joke or give a quick hug. Those continual reminders throughout the day are "love notes" we send our children. Being alert for love notes from God helps us remember His love for us.

Bringing It Home

- Having "joy in the journey" is possible because we are confident we will live forever in heaven with Jesus.

- We are "Easter people," who rejoice every day, knowing that Jesus has rescued us from our slavery to sin.

Let's Remember

I, the LORD your God, hold your right hand; it is I who say to you, "Fear not, I am the one who helps you."
Isaiah 41:13

Masks

Carlos and Gabriella stood on the other side of the basement as the worker flipped down his mask to cover his face. Using a torch, he soldered together shiny metal pieces. Satisfied, he took off the headgear.

"I saw a scary mask on Halloween," said Gabriella.

"It wasn't scary," said Carlos.

Turning to the children, the worker explained, "This mask protects my face when I'm working."

"Firefighters wear masks sometimes," said Carlos. "I know all about firemen."

The two children had been in the basement all morning, just watching. First, the workers had taken out the old furnace. Dirt flew all over. Gabriella had covered her ears at the loud noise. Now, the workers were installing new equipment.

"I'm going to be a firefighter when I grow up," said Carlos. "I'll wear a mask when I rescue people from smoky houses."

Gabriella decided she did not want to wear a mask when she grew up. She thought a mask might be scary to little children.

Dear God,

Thank You for people who fix things in our houses. Thank You for other workers who help us, like _____. Thank You, in Jesus' name. Amen.

Let's Talk

Why had the children stayed in the basement? When people wear a mask, how can they see? Have you ever worn a mask?

Let's Remember
You visit the earth and water it;
You greatly enrich it. Psalm 65:9

Singing Glasses

"I'm starved," said Gianna.

"Lunch will be ready in a few minutes," said her mom. "Drink some milk while you're waiting."

Gianna sipped from her glass, then started tapping the glass with her fork. It sounded like a bell. She drank a little more milk, then tapped again. The sound was different.

Gianna opened a cabinet and took out several more glasses. Then she added water to each glass. She filled up one glass to the top and left another almost empty. When the glasses were lined up in a row, she tapped each one.

"I hear your singing glasses," said her mom, bringing lunch to the table.

"Whoops!" said Gianna as her finger slipped into the full glass of water. She ran her wet finger along the rim of the glass and listened as her finger made a ringing sound.

"That's enough," said her mom. "Lunch is ready."

Let's Talk

What did Gianna do while she was waiting for lunch? What else could Gianna find in the kitchen that might make music? What do you do while you're waiting before a meal?

Dear God,

Thank You for water. I drink it, splash in it, and _____. Thank You for putting water on this earth. Thank You for my Savior, Jesus. In His name. Amen.

Parent Connection

Children misbehave most often when they are tired, hungry, or thirsty. This is why the half hour before a meal triggers the least compliant behavior. Avoid problems by stashing small toys in a kitchen drawer or cabinet. The items can be odds and ends leftover from games, scraps of fabric, scrap-booking paper, or anything that might keep your child occupied during those awkward moments just before mealtime.

Bringing It Home

• We can join with our child and sing that "Jesus loves me" because "the Bible tells me so."

• In Baptism, the water and the Word wash us clean of sin and unite us with Jesus.

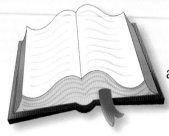

Let's Remember

He [the LORD] will command His
angels concerning you to guard you
in all your ways. Psalm 91:11

Snow Angels

Grace and her grandpa trudged through the snow. They were looking for the perfect spot. The snow needed to be pure and light. Most important, no one could have walked there.

"I see it," pointed Grace. "That's a perfect place."

An entire field, covered in snow, lay before them.

"I'll go first," said her grandpa. "I'll take small steps so you can follow in my footprints."

Grace walked cautiously. Then Grandpa said for her to stop and wait. She watched as Grandpa fell backward into the snow. *Kerplatch!* He spread out his arms, then swept them up and down. Next, he spread his legs far apart, then brought them together. He moved them back and forth. He sat up, then slowly stood without putting his hands down in the snow.

Retracing his steps, he reached for the spray bottle of colored water that Grace carried in her mittened hands. Grandpa sprayed the impression he had left on the snowy field.

"A pink angel!" Grace said, clapping her mittens together. "You made a pink angel! I want to do it too!"

"We can make a whole chorus of angels," said her grandpa. "Just like in the Bible."

Let's Talk

Grace and her grandfather made snow angels. We read in the Bible that God sends real angels to watch over us and give us important messages. How do you feel about that?

Parent Connection

The image of an angel watching over a sleeping child has been illustrated by countless artists. There are few pictures more comforting for a parent. At a time when outside influences enter our homes through all types of digital images, the words of the psalmist remind us that God's angels stand on guard.

Bringing It Home

- Angels appear in many places in the Bible. The angel Gabriel announced that Jesus would be born, and the angels at the tomb told of His resurrection.

- God sends His angels to protect us and our families. We can be sure that through Jesus, God protects us from sin, death, and the devil.

Stormy Seas

Hailey moved her hands through the water. *Swish, swish!* Water splashed on the sides of the tub. Her red boat rocked back and forth, to and fro, as Hailey made waves.

"The water swirled around, and the men were so afraid," she said. "The water roared like thunder."

She pushed the water still harder, rocking the boat even more.

" 'Be still,' " she said. "Jesus said, 'Be still.' "

She took her hands out of the water, and the waves stopped. The tub water settled around the little plastic boat. All was quiet.

Mommy clapped.

"That was a very good retelling of the Sunday School lesson," said her mother. "You showed exactly how Jesus calmed the storm."

"I want to do it again," said Hailey.

"Okay," said her mom. "But let's add a little more warm water. The lake temperature is getting too cool!"

Let's Talk

What did Hailey use to act out the story of Jesus calming the storm (Mark 4:35–41)? What would you need to tell the story of the first Christmas (Luke 2:1–7)? What other Bible stories would be fun to act out?

Parent Connection

Although children often use miniature fire engines or farm animals in their play, we seldom encourage acting out Bible stories. And yet, we know that play is the work of childhood. Retelling a Bible story through dramatic play, as in this example, is one of the most effective ways for a child to learn biblical truths. When the story is appropriate, after your child hears a Bible story, encourage her to re-enact key points while she describes the action.

Bringing It Home

• The Bible records many miracles Jesus performed during His time on earth.

• The greatest miracle is that Jesus died on the cross to forgive our sins and then rose again from the grave.

99

Let's Remember

Lay up for yourselves treasures
in heaven. Matthew 6:20

Treasures

"What are you doing?" yelled Jeremiah.

Hannah looked up. She was sitting in front of an open drawer in her brother's bedroom. Jeremiah called it his "treasure drawer."

"Get out of here!" he yelled. "Get out!"

Hannah ran out of the room, crying, "Jeremiah yelled at me!"

Jeremiah settled on the floor in front of the drawer. He carefully put the treasures back into the drawer: the stick he had found at the park, a blue plastic ring from a birthday party, and his favorite toy trucks. Then he slid the drawer shut.

"What's all the commotion?" asked their mother, coming into the room with a sobbing Hannah close behind her.

"She got into my special drawer!" said Jeremiah. "Those are my treasures."

What do you think happened next?

Dear God,

Thank You for giving me so many things to play with. My favorite toys are _____. Thank You for sending Jesus to be my Savior. In His name. Amen.

Let's Talk

A treasure can be anything that is important to you. A treasure does not always cost a lot of money. Do you keep treasures in a special place? What two items are most important to you?

Parent Connection

Competition for a parent's attention is a frequent cause of conflict between siblings. But disagreements also commonly erupt over issues related to possessions or personal space. Reduce these conflicts by making sure each child has a designated space for valued objects, then enforce those boundaries. Children who learn to respect people and belongings in their early years are less likely to violate privacy, speak rudely, or cross these boundaries when they are older.

Bringing It Home

• God gives us what we need, although not always what we want.

• God shows that He treasures us most by sending Jesus as our Savior.

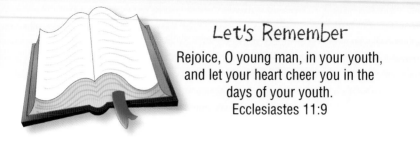

Let's Remember

Rejoice, O young man, in your youth,
and let your heart cheer you in the
days of your youth.
Ecclesiastes 11:9

Snuggle Mountain

Henry raced down the hallway. Then he took a running leap. *Plop!* He landed right in the middle of the laundry basket that was overflowing with warm clothes.

"Henry, what are you doing?" asked his mom. "I just took that load out of the dryer."

"I know," said a muffled voice from deep within the basket. "I'm buried in Snuggle Mountain."

"Those clothes were all clean," warned his mom. Henry's head popped up. Some of his hair stood straight up. He peeked out from the laundry.

Dear God,

Thank You for ____, who washes my clothes. Thank You for ___, who tucks me into bed. Thank You for Jesus, who loves me too. In His name. Amen.

"Snuggle Mountain is nice and warm," said Henry. "I like nice and warm. And it smells good too."

Let's Talk

Who does your laundry? Who folds the clean clothes and puts them away? The next time you see those people, what would you like to tell them?

Parent Connection

On a busy day when laundry is only one of many tasks, we would probably not even think of labeling a basket of clean laundry "Snuggle Mountain." One of the great joys of parenting is seeing the world through a child's filter. Take time today to look through your child's eyes and enjoy life from his perspective.

Bringing It Home

- Satisfaction from our vocation (our job or role in life) comes from doing what God has asked us to do.

- Jesus' job was to teach about God's kingdom and save us from our sins by dying on the cross.

Fireworks

Brooklyn had been looking forward to this day for a very long time. Her family was going to a festival and then staying to watch the fireworks. The fireworks didn't start until dark, so she would stay up past bedtime.

Before leaving for the festival, Brooklyn's dad said, "I want to talk with you."

Brooklyn was so excited, she could barely settle down.

"There will be more people there than you've ever seen," he said.

Brooklyn nodded and said, "A huge crowd."

"Yes," he said. "I want you to stay right next to me and your mom. But if we get separated, go to someone wearing a uniform. Tell that person that you are lost."

Brooklyn's eyes got very big. She said, "Will I get lost?"

Her dad said, "We'll be next to you the whole time, but

Dear God,

Thank You for people like _____ who love me and take care of me. I know You take care of me too. Thank You, God! In Jesus' name. Amen.

sometimes people push and shove in crowds. You need to know what to do if you get separated from us."

Brooklyn nodded, but she didn't say anything.

Soon it was time to leave for the festival. Brooklyn dragged her feet. She wasn't sure she wanted to go.

"Come on, Honey," said her dad.

Brooklyn said, "Maybe we should stay home."

"What?" asked her dad.

Brooklyn said, "I don't want to get lost."

Her dad put his arm around her. "Mommy and I will be right next to you. You'll be safe."

Let's Talk

Why was Brooklyn worried about going to the festival? Who has stayed next to you in a big crowd?

Let's Remember

God is our refuge and strength,
a very present help in trouble.
Psalm 46:1

Rattle, Rattle

Rattle, rattle.

"What's that noise, Mommy?" Hunter asked.

Hunter looked in the car mirror that hung above the driver's seat. He could only see her forehead, but he knew his mother was frowning.

"I don't know," she said. She sounded concerned.

Rattle, rattle. There was that sound again.

"What's making that noise?" Hunter asked again.

"I'm not sure," his mom said. "Please be quiet and let me listen."

The rattle was louder this time.

"It sounds like part of the car is going to fall off," said Hunter. "What's going to happen?"

His mom was quiet. The car rattled as it continued down the street. Hunter heard the *click, click* of the signal light as his mom pulled into a parking lot. Hunter felt like crying.

"Let me think," said his mom. "We can try to make it home. Or . . . "

"I have an idea," interrupted Hunter.

What do you think Hunter suggested?

Dear God,

When I have a problem, I know I can always talk to You. I pray to You in Jesus' name. **Amen.**

Let's Talk

There are often several ways to solve a problem. Talk about a problem you solved.

Parent Connection

Young children are imitators. Being copycats is part of who they are. This is one of the ways they learn. Therefore, without giving your little one intentional lessons, you are helping her learn to solve problems. She can learn even more beneficial life lessons when you specifically show her how to handle a situation. As you identify a problem, suggest several solutions, then apply the best solution. Following this template is effective for parents and children.

Bringing It Home

- Whether we face a major issue or a minor problem, God always listens to us when we pray in Jesus' name.

- When we are uncertain about what to pray, we can pray the Lord's Prayer, and we can be assured that the Holy Spirit prays for us.

Let's Remember

Four things on earth are small, but
they are exceedingly wise.
Proverbs 30:24

Busy Workers

Isaac used a stick to poke at the crack in the sidewalk. Mud flew up, almost hitting Jasmine.

"Don't do that," she said, brushing away bits of mud that had landed nearby.

"Look, Jas," Isaac said. "Look at this."

Bending so low that his nose almost touched the sidewalk, Isaac could see what looked like an army of ants. Some were carrying things. Others were merely walking around.

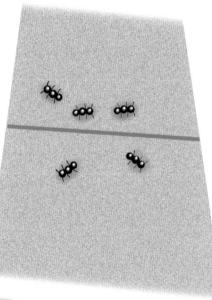

"Those are just ants," said Jasmine. "Let's go swing."

Jasmine headed for the swings while Isaac almost buried his nose in the ant army.

"What are you doing down there?" his mom asked Isaac.

"I found ants," he replied.

His mom crouched next to him.

Dear God,

When I think that You created even tiny insects like ants, I want to tell You _____ . In Jesus' name. Amen.

"It looks like you found a whole colony," she said. "Ants are amazing. They don't have ears, but they feel vibrations through their feet."

Isaac jumped up and down.

"Like this?" he asked.

"You've scared them now, but they'll come back if they have a job to do," said his mom. "The Bible says they work hard."

Isaac looked at the ants scurrying around. "Ants are in the Bible?"

She nodded. "Lots of animals are."

Let's Talk

What were the ants doing? How many of the animals mentioned in the following Bible passages have you seen? See Proverbs 6:6–8; 1 Kings 10:22; Psalm 118:12; and Leviticus 11:15-20, 22, 29–30.

Let's Remember

In peace I will both lie down and sleep; for You alone, O Lord, make me dwell in safety. Psalm 4:8

Sounds of the Night

Chirp, chirp, chirp.

"What's that sound?" asked Emma. She listened with her grandma: *chirp, chirp, chirp.*

"That sounds like a cricket chirping a lullaby," said her grandma.

Whoo, whoo. Emma listened with her grandma: *whoo, whoo.*

"What's that sound?" asked Emma.

"That sounds like an owl saying, 'Good night, sleep tight,'" said her grandma.

Then Emma heard soft humming. *Hmmm, hmmm.*

"What's that sound, Grandma?" she asked.

"That is Grandma telling you it's time to close your eyes," smiled her grandmother. "Let the sounds of the night sing you to sleep."

Let's Talk

Who was the last person to talk to Emma before she fell asleep? Do you hear the same sounds Emma heard, or do you hear different sounds when you go to bed? Who is the last person you talk with before falling asleep?

Dear God

Please watch over me when I sleep.
Please bless everyone I love too,
including ____. In Jesus' name.
Amen.

Parent Connection

Familiar household sounds are often comforting to a child as he drifts to sleep. Before he climbs into bed in an unfamiliar place, help your child identify the new sounds he hears. When he knows what is making the noises, he will be less likely to imagine frightening things that could keep him awake.

Bringing It Home

- We can feel safe when we go to sleep, because God never sleeps; He is always watching over us.

- The safe place we can always count on is the place Jesus secures for us in heaven.

Moon Talk

Isabella leaned on the windowsill. Up in the sky, the moon looked very big. It was so round. It shone like a giant white ball.

"Daddy, come quick," she said. "The moon is smiling."

Her dad peered over her shoulder.

"That's the man in the moon," he explained.

"There's a man inside the moon?" Isabella asked. "Did God put him there?"

"Long ago, when God made the moon, He created hills and valleys on it," her dad said. "That's the reason some areas look light and some areas look dark."

Isabella studied the moon. She could see the dark shadows, but now she couldn't see the smiling face!

"Some people think they see a man carrying a backpack," her dad said. "Other people imagine a girl and a big rabbit."

"But all we really see are just shadows caused by high and low places," Isabella said.

"That's right," said her dad. "Unless an astronaut has landed on a moon mission, there is no person on the moon. Just a lot of rocks."

Isabella thought about that for a very long time.

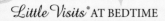

Dear God,

I know You created everything in this whole wide world, even the moon. The next time I look up at the moon, I will _____. In Jesus' name. Amen.

Let's Talk

Why did Isabella think there was a man in the moon? Astronauts have brought rocks back from the moon. What would you do with a moon rock?

Let's Remember

To the snow [God] says, "Fall on the earth." Job 37:6

Awesome

When he woke this morning, Jack could tell this would be a great day: the ground was completely white. More snow was falling. After a quick breakfast, he pulled on snow pants, boots, mittens, a hat, and his warmest coat.

When Jack stepped outside, he opened his mouth and stuck out his tongue. Snowflakes fell right into his mouth! Brrr! That air felt cold. When he held out his hands, snowflakes landed on his mittens.

Then he started to build a snowman. The little snowball started to get so big that Jack could hardly move it. Jack's friend Evan trudged through the snow to help.

"Thanks," said Jack. Then they rolled another ball. They struggled to lift it up. This snowman was going to have a big body.

Dear God,

Thank You, God, for snow. Snow
_____. In Jesus' name.
Amen.

"Jack, time to come in," he heard from a distance.

Jack patted his wet mittens and said to Evan, "Gotta go. I'll ask my mom if we can make snow candy after lunch."

As he opened the back door, warm air poured out. Jack called, "Mom, you gotta come see this."

Shivering, his mom stood in the doorway. Together they watched the snowflakes, each so perfect, land on Jack's wet mittens.

"God does the awesomest things," said his mom.

Let's Talk

What did Jack do in the snow? What awesome thing do you think Jack's mom was talking about?

Parent Connection

Adults see snow as beautiful, but they also consider what comes with it: traffic hazards and hours of shoveling. Children, however, see the pure beauty. Snow even tastes good! To make snow candy, ask your child to firmly pack fresh, clean snow into a pie pan. Keep the pan in the freezer while you bring real maple syrup to a boil on the stove. When the syrup reaches the soft ball stage, drizzle it over the frozen pan of snow. Let the syrup cool briefly before eating the snow candy.

Bringing It Home

- Every snowflake, like every child, is different; yet every person is the same in one way: we all need a Savior from our sin.

- God continues to amaze us with His awesome creation and His love for us.

Let's Remember

The name of the LORD is a strong
tower; the righteous man runs into
it and is safe. Proverbs 18:10

The New Boy

"Come on, Angel," said Robert. "I want you to meet my new friend. He's the coolest guy and has the neatest games."

The boys headed down the sidewalk.

Robert said, "He just moved here, so he doesn't have any friends. I told him he could join our club."

Big brown packing boxes still littered the lawn as the boys walked up the front stairs. The door was propped open, but Robert still rang the doorbell.

A tall, thin boy came to the door.

"Hi," said Robert. "This is Angel, the friend I told you about."

The new boy looked at Angel, frowned, and said, "Angel? *Angel?* What kind of a name is that?"

Robert and Angel didn't know what to say. What would you have said?

Let's Talk

Do you think the new boy will make a lot of friends? What do you like to play with your friends?

Dear God,

Thank You for friends, especially _____. Thank You for our best friend, Jesus. In His name. Amen.

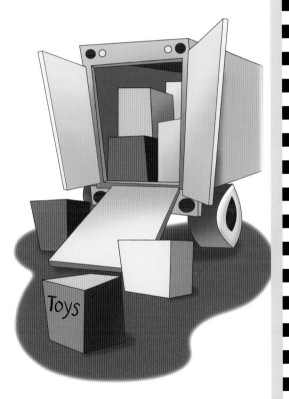

Toys

Parent Connection

Children are not born knowing how to make friends. Parents must teach a child how to make a friend, be a friend, and keep a friend. Research shows that children who spend a great deal of time in front of a screen might need extra help in learning how to make eye contact and read body language. Informally assess the real-time communication skills your child uses in social settings: can he initiate, continue, and close a conversation that lasts at least 30 seconds?

Bringing It Home

- It is because God makes us feel special by His great gift of unending love that we can show that love to others.

- Being called "Christian" means we believe in Jesus Christ as our Savior.

Let's Remember

Let the wise hear and increase
in learning. Proverbs 1:5

A Surprising Day

Jason dragged his feet. He didn't want to go to the museum. His whole family was going, but Jason wanted to stay home and play with his toy astronauts.

The museum parking lot was huge. Jason was tired of walking by the time they reached the museum entrance. He was surprised to see a rocket ship by the information desk. Inside the rocket, he could see the wires, switches, and levers. That was neat.

His sister wanted to see a big dollhouse in the basement of the museum. Jason knew that would be boring—but near the dollhouse, he saw a penny drop. When Jason dropped a penny in the slot, it circled around and around and around before falling to the bottom. Jason was surprised when his dad gave him six more pennies to drop. Jason thought that was really fun.

His brother wanted to see the big model train exhibit. Jason was surprised at how many trains could run on the different tracks at the same time. He liked that.

At lunch, Jason chose what he wanted to eat from a big menu on the wall. Jason ordered spaghetti with meatballs. He was surprised the meatballs were so big. He ate his whole meal.

What a surprising day!

Dear God,

I pray to You in Jesus' name. I know You love me. That's no surprise!
Amen.

Let's Talk

Why didn't Jason want to go to the museum? What museum do you like to visit? A surprise is something we don't expect. When have you been surprised?

Parent Connection

When children have a negative response or reaction to a new situation, it is generally because of what they've seen, heard, or imagined. After all, their base of experiences is quite limited. Anticipating a public scene, parents are often reluctant to insist a child try something new. But providing multiple interactions with people, places, and ideas builds an essential foundation for living in the 21st century.

Bringing It Home

- The Bible tells us that Jesus did many things that surprised people.
- We surprise others by forgiving them, as Jesus did by dying for our sins.

119

Listen Up!

Connor was having a great time at the park. He scrambled up the ladder and then zipped down the slide again and again. Up and down, up and down, faster and faster he ran between the pieces of equipment.

"Connor, it's time to leave," called his mom from the park bench.

Connor pretended not to hear. Up and down he went.

"Connor, we need to pick up your brother," called his mom. Connor held his hands over his ears. Then he pulled down the baseball cap so he couldn't hear as well. He hopped onto a swing and started to pump. Higher and higher he went.

"Connor?" his mother called.

"I can't hear you," he called back. "I'm swinging."

His mother walked over to the swings. What do you think happened next?

Let's Talk

The Bible says that children should obey their parents. What does *obey* mean? In this story, was Connor being obedient?

Dear God,

I know I should obey, but sometimes I don't. When I don't obey, I _____. I know that Jesus forgives my sin. In His name. **Amen.**

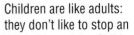

Parent Connection

Children are like adults: they don't like to stop an enjoyable activity. Children, like adults, also respond better when they have time to emotionally and mentally transition to closure. If the mom in this story had given her son a warning five minutes before it was time to leave, would he have obeyed? We don't know, but we do know that preparing children for change is the most effective first step to a smooth transition.

Bringing It Home

- Perfect obedience is impossible because we all sin. Only Jesus was perfect.

- Because of Jesus and His perfect sacrifice on the cross, we are forgiven.

Let's Remember

The righteous is generous and gives.
Psalm 37:21

The Best Seat

"Wash up, everybody," Grandpa called from the kitchen. "It's almost time to eat."

Jennifer had washed her hands earlier, waiting for this moment. She planned to get the best seat, directly in front of the pink cherry salad. Jennifer didn't just *like* cherries. Jennifer *loved* the bright red cherries Grandpa put on top of the holiday salad. Last year, Jennifer only got a couple of cherries. This year, she planned to sit directly in front of the bowl and grab every single one.

"Let's thank God for our blessings," called Grandpa. Everyone held hands to pray. Daisy, Grandpa's dog, ran around the circle, yipping as they prayed. "Amen," said Grandpa.

Jennifer zoomed into the dining room to scan the table, which was loaded with all types of dishes. She scooted into the chair in front of the bright red cherries atop the pink salad.

Dear God,

Sometimes it is so hard to share. Please help me be kind. I pray to You in Jesus' name. **Amen.**

Parent Connection

Coping with disappointment is difficult at any age, but especially so for a child. He does not have the range of experiences to put a single situation into a wider perspective or to know that disappointments are a part of life. In this story, Jennifer's parents might have no idea that the reason for her unhappy state could be traced to the fact that, as the old axiom says, life is not a bowl of cherries. When you don't know the reason for your child's behavior, seek to identify the root cause, and help him learn to cope with the emotion.

Her aunt settled a little cousin into a booster seat next to Jennifer.

"Eeee!" squealed the little girl, pointing to the cherries. Jennifer's aunt spooned off a few cherries and plopped them onto the plate in front of the baby. She stuffed several into her mouth. One cherry fell to the floor. Jennifer quickly counted the cherries left on the salad. There were only seven bright cherries left.

Her aunt pulled a few more cherries off the top as she explained to Jennifer, "Your little cousin is just learning how to eat, but she seems to love these cherries."

What do you think Jennifer said?

Let's Talk

Why was Jennifer eager to get to the table? Did she get the best seat?

Bringing It Home

- Sharing God's Good News that Jesus is our risen Savior goes beyond a natural expression of generosity: it is central to our role as Christian parents.

- True generosity flows out of God's love through us.

Let's Remember

I praise You, for I am fearfully and
wonderfully made. Psalm 139:14

A Good Fit?

John's mother added another T-shirt to the stack. The stack
of shirts almost toppled over.

"I want to keep that one," said John, picking up one of the
shirts. He loved the yellow shirt with the red car.

"But it doesn't fit anymore," said his
mom.

John didn't say anything as he
pulled off the shirt he was wearing. He tugged hard to get the
yellow shirt over his head.
It hurt to pull it down over
his ears, but he didn't say
anything.

"See?" John said. "It
fits."

John looked in the
mirror. He could see
that the shirt was too
short. It even felt tight.

Dear God,

Thank You for clothes to wear. My favorite clothes are _____. When my clothes get too small, help me find ways to share them with others.
In Jesus' name. Amen.

"If we keep this shirt, it will just take up room in your drawer," said his mom. "If we give the shirt away, another child will enjoy wearing this yellow shirt with a red car."

John turned away from the mirror. His mom helped him pull off the yellow shirt and put his other shirt back on. "It's no fun to grow up," he mumbled.

Let's Talk

Why were John's clothes too small for him? What could you say to John to help him feel better? What happens to clothes that are too small for you?

Parent Connection

Children are not always happy to reach milestones that are obvious signs of growth: a child might not want to lose a tooth, discard too-small clothes, or move up a grade at school. Even if the situation appears relatively minor, a child will need to grieve, if only briefly, the loss of what he currently has before he can smoothly transition to something new.

Bringing It Home

- The best example of generosity was God's gift of Jesus as our Savior.

- God blesses our generosity by giving us joy through our giving.

Let's Remember

He [the Lord] determines the number
of the stars; He gives to all of them
their names. Psalm 147:4

Star Light, Star Bright

José snuggled into his dad's arms. Every night, the two of them sat by the window at bedtime. In spring, they could barely see the shadow of new leaves in the dim light. In summer, they listened to crickets chirp. In fall, they watched rain pelt against the glass, and in winter, they counted snowflakes drifting down. Tonight they looked straight up at the sky.

"How many stars are there?" José asked.

"On a clear night, we can see about 3,000," said his dad. "With a telescope, we would see 100,000, but there are even more stars than that."

"Are there 10 billion trillion stars?" José asked.

His dad nodded, looking toward one especially bright star. "Yes," he said. "God made at least 10 billion trillion stars. But you know what?"

"What?" asked José.

"The Bible says God not only made the stars and counts the stars, but He also gives them all names," said his dad.

"Wow!" said José. "God is amazing!"

Dear God,

When I think that You created everything in this whole wide world, I want to say _____. In Jesus' name. **Amen.**

Let's Talk

José looked out his bedroom window at night. What do you see outside your window at night? If you could name a star, what would you call it? Why would you give it that name?

Parent Connection

We can easily be overwhelmed when we consider the work of God, our Creator. Yet a child focuses narrowly—on a worm squiggling in her hand or a spider spinning a delicate web. A child sees the wonder of the Creator by focusing on a single element. Today, look through your child's lens and enjoy the majesty of God's creation.

Bringing It Home

• As Creator of the universe, God made a special star for the Wise Men to follow across many miles and months so they could worship Jesus.

• Instead of wishing on a star, we pray to God in Jesus' name, confident that He hears us and answers according to His will for us.

Find a Friend

"Grrrr! Grrrr!" Andrew stalked around the house. He curled his fingers so they looked like claws. "Grrrr! Grrrr!" he said, walking toward his little sister, Elizabeth.

"I'm a scary monster," he growled, taking giant steps.

"Mommy, Mommy!" Elizabeth cried, running to find her mom.

"I'm a scary monster!" Andrew repeated, taking even bigger steps as he walked through the kitchen, then the bathroom, and finally into the living room.

He could barely see Elizabeth, who was hiding behind their mom.

"Andrew, why are you acting like that?" his mom asked.

"I'm in a bad mood," Andrew growled.

"Why are you in a bad mood?" his mom asked.

"Nobody will play with me," said Andrew. "Grrrr! Grrrr!"

Let's Talk

Would you like to play with Andrew when he is acting like that? What do you do when you can't find anyone to play with?

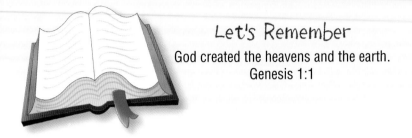

Dirty Gloves

Josh and Nate loved playing with trucks. They used a large front loader to scoop dirt in their digging corner. Then they used a yellow grader to smooth the dirt. Then Nate dug up more dirt with a bulldozer. Today the dirt was really dirty: rain had turned their digging corner into a mud corner. The boys didn't mind though. They still played with their trucks.

"It's getting colder," called their mom. "Do you have gloves?"

"Sure," said Josh.

The boys played a little longer.
When their mom came out to the
mud corner, she scolded, "Josh, you
told me you were wearing gloves."

Josh showed her his mud-covered hands.

"I *am* wearing gloves," he said.
"Mud makes good gloves."

Let's Talk

Do you agree with Josh, that
mud makes good gloves? When do
you wear gloves or mittens?

Footprints

Addison followed her Uncle Matt into the trees behind her house. They were pretending to be explorers.

"Look at this," said Uncle Matt, bending over to inspect a muddy print. "What do you think made this?"

Addison stared at the impression. It was large with a rounded top. The bottom of the print was square.

"That's silly, Uncle Matt," she said. "You made that print. That was your shoe."

Uncle Matt's big laugh echoed through the trees.

"You're right," he said. "But that's the type of print we're searching for. Find a place where something pressed down in the mud."

They walked on, pushing back leaves and branches still dripping from the rain. Addison was so intent on watching the ground for prints that a branch almost hit her in the face.

Dear God,

You gave me my very own fingerprints. I know no one in the whole world has fingerprints like mine. Thank You for making me me. In Jesus' name. Amen.

"Here's one," said Uncle Matt. He pushed back low-hanging leaves. "This animal has four toes, large claws, and a small heel."

"What was it?" Addison asked.

"Probably a dog or a fox," he said. "Let's keep looking."

They found the heart-shaped, two-toed track from a deer. And then they saw what looked like a tiny handprint. Uncle Matt said it was probably from a raccoon.

"This was fun," he said as they headed home. "But we better clean off our shoes before going inside. We don't want to leave tracks on the floor."

Let's Talk

Where could you leave a footprint? Where could you leave a handprint that would easily wash away?

Good Night

Julia shivered, but she wasn't cold. Although she was cozy, all tucked in bed, she remembered a scary picture on television. It had flashed for only a moment before her mom clicked it off, but Julia couldn't get the picture out of her head.

"Ready to pray?" her mom asked, coming into the room.

"I guess so," said Julia, quietly.

"You don't sound very sure," said her mom. "What's the problem? Are your toes tired? Or are your legs tired? Or your knees? Or is your tummy tired?"

Julia giggled as her mom tickled each body part. Then Julia grew serious again.

"Mommy, I keep seeing that icky picture in my head," said Julia. "Even when I close my eyes, it's still there."

"Well then, let's turn to the Farm Channel on Brain TV," said her mom.

Her mom started to describe some of the animals they had seen on a farm, especially the brown horse with the long tail. Julia smiled as she remembered how the horse nuzzled her fingers as it grabbed a carrot. Then her mom talked about the nine piglets, pushing and shoving and squealing for a place to eat as their mom rooted around in the mud. Julia smiled, then opened her eyes and reached for a hug.

"Thanks, Mommy," she said. "Now I'll try to picture the rooster that kept crowing."

Her mom smiled and said, "And then we'll ask God to give you good dreams."

Let's Talk

Why was Julia having trouble getting to sleep? What do you do when you have a bad dream? Describe a good dream you've had.

Parent Connection

An image that flashes on a screen, an accident on the highway, or a child's runaway imagination of spiders and bad guys can trigger bad dreams. A technique used in this story—to change the mental picture—empowers a child to shift away from feeling like a victim. During the final hour before bedtime, turn off all outside influences and focus inward on your family and God's blessings. This invites your child to settle into a reassuring and familiar cocoon before falling asleep.

Bringing It Home

• The apostle Paul encourages us to think good thoughts (Philippians 4:8), and we will have the peace of God.

• By focusing on Jesus and His mercy for us, troubling ideas that otherwise disturb us will fall away so we can drift into a peaceful sleep.

Let's Remember

May the whole earth be filled
with His glory! Psalm 72:19

Spring Has Sprung

Luis held tightly to the leash. Sparky trotted alongside, stopping to inspect every blade of green that had popped up after the morning shower. During several days of rain, buds had popped out on the fragrant bushes. Now Sparky had so many new things to sniff! Everything smelled clean and fresh.

Luis thought he could smell lasagna, but perhaps that was his imagination. He knew Grandpa was busy in the kitchen, but Luis didn't think he would be able to smell the rich tomato sauce and spices from so far away. Still, Luis walked faster as his nose started to twitch, and his tummy rumbled at the thought of supper.

Sparky started running as his short legs tried to keep up with the hungry boy. Running up the back stairs, Luis opened the door. Sparky barked a greeting to Grandpa and dashed inside. As Luis hung up Sparky's leash, he breathed deeply of the supper in the oven. He knew the lasagna would taste just as good as it smelled.

Dear God,

I don't often think about my nose, but I'm so glad I can smell. Thank You for giving me such a good nose. In Jesus' name. Amen.

Let's Talk

Who was more eager to get home: Sparky or Luis? What can you smell in spring that you can't smell in winter?

Parent Connection

As a newborn, your infant depended on his nose, not his eyes or ears, to identify you. The olfactory sense is the most advanced of the five senses at birth. Research shows the ability to identify odors plateaus at about age 8, then can decline as people grow older. Give your house the sniff test: ask your child what the various rooms smell like. You might be surprised!

Bringing It Home

- The Bible says that when we please God, our actions smell sweet to Him (2 Corinthians 2:15).

- The good things we do for others are an extension of Jesus' ultimate "good thing" He did for us—forgiving our sins so we can be reconciled to God.

Lost and Found

Justin looked under the chair. The wheel wasn't there. Then he moved the stack of papers that were sitting on the floor. The wheel hadn't rolled underneath. Finally, he got a yardstick to reach under the sofa. He found a plastic ring from a birthday party and some fish-shaped crackers, but not the missing wheel. How far had it rolled?

Justin was still upset, but he went back to playing. Yet all afternoon, he wondered, *Where did the wheel go?*

Dear God,

When I misplace something, I get angry or upset. When I'm bothered like that, help me remember _____. In Jesus' name. Amen.

At supper, he asked his family, "Have you seen my wheel?"

But no one had seen the small, black wheel that belonged on the car.

After supper, his mother called from the kitchen, "Justin, could you come here please? Something is under my foot."

What do you think his mom stepped on?

Let's Talk

In the Bible, read Luke 15:8–9, which tells about a woman who lost money. In this Bible story, the woman "rejoiced" when she found her coin. Do you think Justin rejoiced when he found his wheel?

Parent Connection

Very young children do not have impulse control to manage strong emotions like anger and frustration. But as children develop more language skills, we can remind them to "use your words" to express their emotions. Children who listen as you use language to cope with your own problems will learn socially acceptable ways to show how they feel.

Bringing It Home

- We were lost in our sins until Jesus found us. Jesus continues to search for us when we wander away from Him.

- God the Father and all of heaven rejoice when we stop sinning and return to Him.

A Disappointing Day?

Kaitlin was so disappointed. All her friends had been invited to Rachel's party. Everyone except Kaitlin. She felt tears drip down her cheeks. As she sat on the sofa and cried, Tiger jumped up and stood in her lap.

"Your fur will get all wet, Tiger," Kaitlyn sobbed, but the kitty didn't seem to mind. Tiger curled up and went to sleep.

Hearing Kaitlyn talking to Tiger, her mom came into the room.

"Well, that's one happy cat," said her mom. Then, looking more closely, her mom asked, "Are you crying?"

Kaitlyn nodded and told the sad story: everyone else had been invited to Rachel's party—everyone except her.

"When is the party?" asked her mom.

"Saturday afternoon," Kaitlyn said.

"Maybe we can do something special that day," her mom said. "We could bake cookies or go to the library."

Kaitlyn used a tissue to wipe the tears off her face. She thought about her mom's ideas. "Maybe we could do both. We could go to the library first and then come home to bake cookies," said Kaitlyn.

Her mom nodded. "That sounds like a good plan."

Let's Talk

When something doesn't happen that you want to happen, you feel disappointed. The title of this story is a question for you to answer: was this a disappointing day for Kaitlin? When have you been disappointed?

Parent Connection

A child's social disappointment can become a bad memory that lasts a lifetime. To help a child avoid being hurt in this way, sometimes we are over-protective. That's understandable; we hurt for and with our child, so the feeling is intense. But instead of repeatedly shielding a child from such issues, it is healthier to help a child learn to cope with these situations. Empathize with your child, then help her move forward.

Bringing It Home

- Even if we are disappointed, God knows what is best for us.

- Although sin hurts and angers God, He looks at us through the "cross eyes" of Jesus as His forgiven children.

Learning to Wait

Kevin could see for miles as he and his family stood at the scenic overlook. Kevin saw a lake with some houses, fields, and lots of trees. It was very pretty.

But the only thing Kevin could do was look. There was nothing else to do.

"Let's go," he said, grabbing his dad's elbow.

"Not yet," said his dad, unzipping the camera case. "This is a great place for a family photo."

Kevin frowned, but he stood between his older sisters while another tourist snapped a picture of their whole family.

"Let's go now," said Kevin.

"Not yet," said his dad. "I want to read the maps and signs that show what we're seeing."

Kevin started kicking little pebbles that covered the ground.

"Ouch!" whined his oldest sister as a pebble hit her leg.

Their dad turned around.

"Kevin, do you know what it means to be patient?" his dad asked.

"It means you have to wait," said Kevin.

Dear God,

Sometimes when I have to wait,
I _____. Help me to be patient.
In Jesus' name. Amen.

"That's right," said his dad. "Now is a good time for you to practice patience."

Let's Talk

Why was Kevin bored? What else could Kevin have done? Why is it sometimes hard to be patient?

Parent Connection

Learning to wait without whining or fussing is easier for a child who has practiced patience. Initial lessons are most effective when a child is rewarded for waiting. For example, if a child helps make pudding, he knows he can eat the finished product after a few minutes. Spending time when you are focused specifically on him can also be a reward. Perhaps you play I Spy or make up goofy rhymes while waiting in line at the store. Such simple games demonstrate to a child that he can learn to wait.

Bringing It Home

- God's people waited thousands of years for the first Christmas. Only God knew when the Messiah would come.

- Forgiveness through Christ Jesus is His gift to us every day.

Let's Remember

Heal me, O LORD, and I shall
be healed. Jeremiah 17:14

A Feel-Bad Day

Jonathan didn't feel well. His head hurt. His eyes itched. His legs felt achy, and he was really, really crabby.

His little brother gently set his favorite truck on Jonathan's bed to play with. Jonathan didn't even smile.

His dad brought him something to drink, but Jonathan's throat hurt so badly that he didn't drink much.

His mom baked a batch of his favorite cookies, but Jonathan wasn't hungry.

"I don't feel well," he said. "Nothing feels well."

Jonathan started to cry. His mom helped him get dressed, then his dad drove him to the doctor's office. What do you think happened next?

Let's Talk

Why did Jonathan's dad take him to the doctor? Who cares for you when you are sick?

Dear God,

When I don't feel well, thank You for people who take care of me, like _____. I pray this in Jesus' name. **Amen.**

Parent Connection

Like adults, children are cranky when they are sick. But unlike adults, children get sick very quickly and usually recover just as fast. However, in addition to physical aches and pains, a sick child is often afraid. This can increase the intensity of discomfort. Your calm presence and reassuring tone, along with competent medical care, will be most helpful to a sick child.

Bringing It Home

- God sends people into our lives to help us.

- When we help others, we are like Jesus, who, by suffering and dying for us on the cross, healed our worst sickness—sinfulness.

Happy Half

"Happy half-birthday, Lauren," said Grandma.

Lauren was just waking up, so she wasn't sure she heard correctly.

"It's not my birthday," said Lauren, stretching her arms.

"But it's your half-birthday," said Grandma. "Your birthday is in exactly six months, so today is your half-birthday."

"Do I get presents?" asked Lauren.

"We'll see," said Grandma. "This will be a fun day."

For breakfast, Grandma sliced toast into halves. Lauren spread one half with jelly and the other half with honey.

"Yum," said Lauren.

Then Lauren and Grandma used one color of fingernail polish on one hand and a different

Dear God,

Thank You for people who help me have fun. Thank You especially for _____. Thank You, in Jesus' name. Amen.

color on the other hand. They polished only half of their toenails. For lunch, they stuffed pita halves with egg salad. Then they dipped pretzel sticks halfway into melted chocolate.

When the day was half over, Grandma said, "Lauren, it's your half-birthday, but I want to thank God with a whole prayer. You are such a blessing in my life."

Let's Talk

Find your birthday on the calendar. Then count exactly six months from your birthday. That is your half- birthday. What would you like to do on your half-birthday?

Parent Connection

In this story, a half-birthday offered an opportunity to thank God, but we don't need an excuse to do that. God is with us on every step of our parenting journey. During difficult times, God invites us to lean on Him, for He will help carry our load. And during less intense times, God is ready to hear our thanks and praise for His many gifts.

Bringing It Home

• We can't help but thank God for the many ways He blesses us.

• Our greatest blessing is that Jesus paid for all our sins on the cross.

Polka-Dot Grandma

Leah rubbed her grandma's arm.

"Grandma, why does your arm have brown polka dots?"

Her grandmother looked down to see where Leah pointed.

"Those polka dots are called 'age spots,'" her grandma explained.

Then Leah traced blue lines on her grandma's hands. Without waiting for Leah to ask, her grandmother explained, "Those lines are blood vessels. Older people have thin skin, so you can see their blood vessels. You can't see your blood vessels because you have young skin."

Leah inspected her own hands and arms. Grandma was right. Leah couldn't see any blood vessels, and she didn't find a single brown polka dot.

"Is your face wrinkled because you're old?" Leah asked.

"My face is wrinkled because I didn't trust God enough," her grandma said. "Those wrinkles are worry lines."

"Are you getting more wrinkles?" said Leah.

Her grandmother shook her head.

Dear God,

Sometimes I worry. Help me remember not to worry because You love me and send people who love me and take care of me. In Jesus' name. Amen.

"Not anymore," she said. "I trust God to take care of me, even if I am a polka-dot grandma."

Let's Talk

Do all older people have white hair and polka-dot skin? What do you worry about? Do you tell God about your worries?

Parent Connection

Intergenerational relationships help children visualize life from birth to grave. Older people have wisdom, the depth of knowledge that comes with experience, maturity, and reflection. Because wise people recognize the value of time, they are often willing to invest that time in a child. Support and nurture the relationships your child has with people who have wisdom. That time is precious.

Bringing It Home

- No one is too old or too young to experience the love of God and the forgiveness His Son offers.

- God invites us to pray in His name at all times and in all places.

Let's Remember

He has made everything beautiful
in its time. Ecclesiastes 3:11

A Cool Animal

Liam loved to visit the zoo. He especially liked to watch the bears. They would lumber out of a cave, walk ever so slowly, then take a running dive into a pool. Sometimes a bear would sit up on his back legs and just look around. When that happened, Liam pretended the bear was looking directly at him.

Liam's favorite was the polar bear. His coat was clean and white. And in the summer, when it was hot, Liam liked to watch the polar bears play with big blocks of ice and chomp on giant ice pops. Through the zoo glass, Liam liked to watch the big bears swim like a dog, paddling the water with their paws.

Liam thinks that a polar bear is the coolest animal God created. Do you agree?

Let's Talk

Why do you think Liam's favorite zoo animal is the polar bear? What zoo animal makes you laugh?

Dear God,

Thank You for making so many different kinds of animals. I especially like _____. In Jesus' name. **Amen.**

Parent Connection

Even when children do not live near a zoo or wildlife park, they can learn about unfamiliar animals through books and television programs. Such programs can also present images or situations that are scary to a child. When we watch these programs with our children, they observe our responses. If we say, "I wouldn't want to meet a bear in a forest," a child will not only imagine that scene, but will also pick up on our apprehension. Make every effort to avoid transferring your private fears to your child.

Bringing It Home

- God created everyone and everything for a purpose.
- God sent Jesus with the purpose to teach us, forgive us, and offer us salvation.

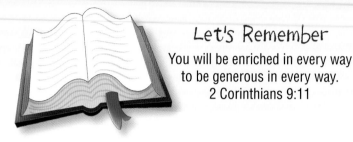

Let's Remember

You will be enriched in every way
to be generous in every way.
2 Corinthians 9:11

More Than Money

Josh shook the money box. He had sold a lot of his old toys at the garage sale. One little boy kept coming back to the same small truck. Josh could tell the little boy really liked the truck. It didn't cost very much, so Josh was certain the boy would buy it. Then Josh would have even more money!

The little boy's mom paid for a huge stack of clothes. She needed two bags for everything she bought. Now she walked over to her son, who waited at the toy table.

"Can we buy this?" the little boy asked.

Setting down the bags, his mom knelt down next to him.

"It's a very nice truck," she said quietly, "but you and your brother need clothes. We don't have extra money to buy toys."

The little boy reached up to set the truck back on the table. Giving the truck just one more look, he turned and walked away with his mom.

Picking up the truck, Josh ran down the driveway toward them.

"Here," said Josh. "You can have this. For free."

Looking up at Josh, the little boy said, "Really?"

Josh nodded.

Dear God,

Help me learn how to give from my
heart. I pray this in Jesus' name.
Amen.

The boy smiled his thanks. Josh
felt good about giving away his truck.

Let's Talk

In this story, Josh was generous.
He gave away his truck because he
wanted to, not because anyone told
him he had to do it. Have you ever
been generous? Has someone been
generous toward you?

Parent Connection

Generosity is a virtue that
emerges over several
years of practice. True
generosity cannot be
forced. We can encour-
age thoughtful giving,
but imposing the action
on our child results not
only in a lack of joy, but
undermines the develop-
ment of generosity and
empathy, or caring for
others. A child who grows
up experiencing the joy of
making a heart connection
through generous giving
will carry that value for a
lifetime.

Bringing It Home

• Money is a blessing
  from God, but we can-
  not buy our entry into
  heaven.

• The Bible says Jesus
  paid for our salvation
  by willingly going to the
  cross on our behalf.

Sounds of the Morning

Logan loved to lie awake in his bed, listening to the sounds of the morning. First he heard the big delivery truck pull up to the store across the street. Sometimes he could hear the grocery cartons clunk onto the dock as they were unloaded.

After that, the garbage truck rumbled in. *Dump, whirr, smash. Dump, whirr, smash.* The sanitation workers emptied garbage into the truck before the cruncher came down and smashed the trash. Logan loved to hear the *dump, whirr, smash.*

Some days, the recycle truck collected bottles, paper, and glass. That's when Logan hopped out of bed. He always looked for the empty containers his family had recycled.

"Logan," called his dad. "Time for breakfast."

That breakfast call was Logan's favorite morning sound.

Dear God,

Sometimes I still feel sleepy when I wake up. Sometimes I hop out of bed and _____. Thank You for this day. In Jesus' name. Amen.

Let's Talk

What sounds did Logan listen to in the morning? What is the first sound you hear when you wake up?

Parent Connection

A child can often predict what kind of day he will have by noticing his parents' morning mood. Even before children learn to read words, they can read emotions. When you make the effort to change your mood from grumpy to happy, you and your child will both enjoy a better day.

Bringing It Home

- Morning is an ideal time to remember that every day is a gift from God.

- Watching the sun rise in the morning is a visual reminder that Jesus rose from the dead and that He offers us eternal life with Him.

Let's Remember

I will send . . . showers of blessing.
Ezekiel 34:26

Showers of Blessings

Matt snuggled down in bed as Grandpa tucked the covers around him. Then Grandpa sat down near Matt's feet.

"It's time to thank God for our blessings," said Grandpa.

"You say that every night," said Matt. "But I don't know what blessings are."

"Blessings are the good things God gives us, everything that's around us," said Grandpa.

Dear God,

Thank You for blessing me in so many ways. Thank You most of all for sending Jesus as my Savior. In His name. Amen.

Matthew looked around, then said, "Like my bed and the rug and the door and the lamp and the waste basket . . ."

"Yes," laughed Grandpa, "even the wastebasket. But blessings are also those breakfast waffles you covered with syrup, and the friends you saw at the park."

"Grandpa, get ready for a long prayer," said Matt. "There were lots of blessings today."

"Matt, God loves to hear you say 'Thank You,' and so do I," smiled Grandpa.

Let's Talk

The Bible tells us that God showers us with blessings. How many blessings did God send you today?

Parent Connection

When we see a child blissfully running through the park or giggling happily at a birthday party, we might think, *He doesn't know how good he has it.* Often, children overflow with sheer happiness. But as we grow older, that joyful experience of waking up eager to begin a new day can be obscured by worries and concerns. Today, thank God for the opportunity to see the world through the lens of a child, for that is truly one of the greatest blessings of life.

Bringing It Home

- God blesses us because He loves us.
- Our greatest blessing is that Jesus is our Savior.

Copycat Kid

Luke was so happy. They were going to his favorite fast food restaurant.

Waiting at the pickup window, his mom called to Luke and Lillian in the backseat. "Do you want chicken nuggets or a hamburger?"

Luke said, "I'll have what Lillian has."

Lillian said, "I'll have nuggets."

"Then I'll have nuggets too," said Luke.

A moment later, their mom asked, "Do you want apple slices or carrots?"

Luke said, "I'll have what Lillian has."

Lillian chose carrots. So Luke wanted those too.

Just as they reached the order taker, their mom called back again, "Milk or apple juice?"

"Apple juice, please," said Lillian.

"Apple juice, please," said Luke.

Lillian glanced over at Luke and asked, "Why are you being a copycat kid?"

Let's Talk

What did Luke order for lunch? Is it good to be a copycat? When have you been a copycat?

Parent Connection

Children imitate to varying degrees. Usually they mimic adults, but they often copy friends or characters they see in media. In this story, Luke might be a "one time only" copycat when he realizes he would have preferred milk to apple juice. Parents would often prefer their child to be a leader, not a follower, but there's a more important message to communicate: be true to who you are as a child of God.

Bringing It Home

• Jesus directed His disciples to "follow Me," so they listened, learned, and then told others what He had taught them. Jesus invites us to follow Him too.

• As imitators of Christ, we show others the same love, forgiveness, and mercy that He first showed us.

Let's Remember

Two are better than one, because they
have a good reward for their toil.
Ecclesiastes 4:9

Picture This

MacKenzie helped her dad push another box out of the garage. She was already hot and sweaty after only a short time.

"We'll *never* get done," she complained. Her dad grunted as the box got caught on a crack in the pavement. Huffing and puffing, he stood and looked back at the garage. They still had to remove the tools before they could turn on the hose to wash away the dirt.

"Come here, MacKenzie," her dad said. He positioned her directly in front of the garage.

"You see the winter's mess and muck in the garage?" he asked. MacKenzie nodded. "Now close your eyes, and imagine how the garage looks when it's been washed out and everything is put away."

MacKenzie squeezed her eyes tight and pictured a sparkling clean garage.

"See how nice it will look?" asked her dad.

"Can we go for ice cream when we're done?" asked MacKenzie, opening her eyes.

"Yes, we can," said her dad. "For now, though, let's get a cool drink and get back to work."

Dear God,

I would rather play than work, but teach me to be a good helper. In Jesus' name. Amen.

Let's Talk

What was MacKenzie doing to help her dad? How did she feel about helping at the beginning of the story? at the end of the story?

Let's Remember

Wash me, and I shall be whiter
than snow. Psalm 51:7

Saying "I'm Sorry"

"Walk, don't run," the lifeguard called.

Katherine slowed to a fast walk. Following right behind her, Madeline was watching only her feet and crashed right into Katherine.

"You messed up our footprints," said Katherine, looking down at the wet pavement.

"Sorry," said Madeline. "This is boring, anyway. Let's do something else."

The girls tossed a beach ball back and forth across the pool. Then they climbed on and off a raft. But when Madeline tried to get on the raft at the same time, Katherine fell into the water.

"Sorry," said Madeline.

"That wasn't much fun, anyway. Let's play something else," said Katherine. The two girls dove for weighted sticks. That was fun—until both girls reached for the same stick at the same time.

"It's mine!" said Madeline.

Dear God,
I need to say "I'm sorry" when I mess up. Thank You for forgiving me. For Jesus' sake. Amen.

"I got it first!" said Katherine.

Madeline let go of the stick and climbed out of the pool. Katherine followed. Madeline sat on a chair, wrapped in a towel. Katherine went up to her and said, "Sorry."

Madeline thought for a moment, then said, "I'm sorry too. Let's go back in the pool. Catch me if you can!"

Let's Talk

Did Madeline and Katherine have a fun day at the pool? Is it easy or hard to tell someone "I'm sorry"?

Parent Connection

Letting go of hurt or anger is not always easy for a child or a parent, but that's the beginning of forgiveness. Forgiveness is closely related to courage, another virtue. It often takes courage to admit what happened and honestly face the truth. If "Sorry" becomes an automatic response, it does not reflect true repentance. Instead of always pushing for an apology, make sure a child understands what he did was wrong and what he should do in the future.

Bringing It Home

• "Repent" means to be truly sorry for our sins and to turn away from them.

• The Bible shows us our sin so we can repent, and points us to forgiveness in Jesus.

Let's Remember

The LORD is near to the brokenhearted
and saves the crushed in spirit.
Psalm 34:18

The Birthday Boy

Ian had been eyeing the big box ever since it arrived. His birthday was still three days away, so he had to wait to open the present. When he talked with Grandma, she wouldn't give a single clue about what was inside, but Ian figured it out.

The box was so huge that Ian thought, *It has to be the excavator I want.* Perhaps he could just tear a little bit of the wrapping paper off the corner to see. But when he did, he could only see some numbers on plain blue cardboard.

Later, Ian thought, *Maybe I'll rip off a tiny piece of paper from another corner. I might be able to see a picture of what's inside.* But he only saw plain blue cardboard.

The next day, Ian ripped off another corner. But his finger accidently made a big tear in the paper. Peeking underneath to see the box, Ian saw a concrete mixer. It was white with blue and yellow stripes, and it was huge. Ian ripped off the rest of the wrapping paper and yelled, "But I wanted an excavator!"

Ian's grandma heard the commotion and came running. She said, "What's wrong?"

What do you think happened next?

Dear God,

Sometimes I disobey. Help me to obey and be thankful for what I have. Through Jesus alone. **Amen.**

Let's Talk

Why didn't Ian wait until his birthday to open the box? Do you think Ian had a happy birthday?

Parent Connection

Learning to obey is one of the hardest lessons for children: there are just so many rules to break and boundaries to be pushed. Young children have not yet developed the impulse control that contributes to learning restraint and results in various levels of self-discipline. At all ages, a child will find it easiest to obey if rules are communicated clearly and enforced consistently.

Bringing It Home

• God's people waited thousands and thousands of years for the Savior to come.

• Waiting is a challenge in today's instant-gratification society, but we no longer need to wait for Jesus: He has already come to be our Savior.

Let's Remember

He gives power to the faint, and
to him who has no might He
increases strength. Isaiah 40:29

Stick with It

The soccer ball rolled slowly across the grass. Then it stopped moving altogether.

"I don't want to practice anymore," complained Madison. Tired, she plopped onto the lawn.

"Come on, Honey," said her dad. "The coach said to practice kicking with the inside of your foot. That's the way real soccer players move the ball."

"I'm tired," whined Madison.

Her dad sat down beside her.

"It's great you want to play on a soccer team," said her dad. "But you need to learn how to kick."

"I'm tired," Madison whined again. "Besides, it's no fun doing the same thing over and over again."

"The first game is Saturday," said her dad. "Your uniform is clean. Your shoes and shin guards fit fine. Grandpa and Grandma are coming to watch the game."

Madison started to stand. "All right," she said. "But practicing isn't much fun."

Dear God,

Learning new things isn't always easy. I worked hard when I was learning to _____. Encourage me to stick with learning new things. In Jesus' name. Amen.

Let's Talk

We often need to practice a skill before we learn to do it well. What skills have you practiced? Riding a bike or scooter? Wrapping a present? Singing a song? Who encourages you to keep trying?

Parent Connection

Teaching perseverance is not easy when instant gratification is built into the culture. And yet, having the determination to see a task through to completion is an important virtue. Instead of rushing in to help a child who's struggling, let your help take the form of encouragement. After all, it's your child, not you, who is learning to play a musical scale or catch a baseball.

Bringing It Home

- After we fall into sin, we get right back up and ask for Jesus' forgiveness.
- Regardless of how many times we break God's commandments, He is always ready to forgive us.

167

Let's Remember

It is good to give thanks to the Lord.
Psalm 92:1

Drawing in the Dust

Mason's dad had asked him to wipe dust off the windows, but he was having more fun drawing pictures on the dirty glass. First he drew a truck with huge wheels. Then he drew a house.

"Mason, you are awfully quiet in there," his dad called. "Grandma will be here soon, and our new house is still filthy."

"I'll dust that round table," said Mason. "There's a lot of dust there."

Mason found so much dust on the table that he could trace a racetrack. Looking past the moving boxes, he saw dust bunnies piled up in a corner. He started blowing them around. He blew and blew until a dust bunny flew up—and landed on top of his dad's shoe.

His dad looked down at Mason. Mason looked up at his dad.

"What are you doing?" his dad asked.

"Having a dust bunny race," Mason said. "And you want to see my racetrack? It's in the dust on that table."

His dad plopped onto the dusty floor and started to laugh. "Mason," he said, reaching out to hug him, "you are such a fun guy. You even make it fun to clean our new, dusty house."

Dear God,

I smile when I get a present, when I get good food to eat, and when I think of all the good things You give me, especially _____. In Jesus' name. Amen.

Let's Talk

Did Mason need a dust cloth? Would Mason be a good helper at your house?

Parent Connection

Children crave our time and attention, so working alongside not only models how to do a job but also offers a bonding opportunity. Arranging parallel job situations is especially important as children get older and communicate less. When a parent and child work side by side, the conversation is not the focal point, but instead, appears merely incidental to the job (even if it's the actual reason we arranged the chore in the first place).

Bringing It Home

- By giving of ourselves, we make the world a better place; by giving up His life, Jesus won our salvation.

- God wants us to respond to His love by sharing His love with others and working to help them.

Promises, Promises

"Mommy," called Lily. Her mom had promised to read an extra story if Lily brushed her teeth, put her clothes in the hamper, and got ready for bed without any reminders. Now Lily was waiting for her story.

"Mommy," she called again. Lily looked around her room as she waited. She loved all her toys, her bed, and even her closet.

As Lily lay in her bed, waiting, she started to get sleepy. She called again, "Mommy, when are you coming? You promised."

"Soon," her mom called back. "I'll be right there."

Lily opened her mouth wide for a big yawn. Then she snuggled down a little deeper under the covers. She had closed her eyes for just a moment when she heard her mom say, "Here I am."

What do you think happened next?

Dear God,

You promised to send Jesus as my Savior, and You did! I know You always keep Your promises. In Jesus' name. **Amen.**

Let's Talk

When you make a promise, you say you will do something. Talk about a time when you made a promise. Talk about a time when someone promised you something.

Let's Remember

Whoever exalts himself will be humbled, and whoever humbles himself will be exalted.

Matthew 23:12

Show-Off

"Show-off, show-off, you're nothing but a show-off!" sang Mia. Leaving Ella behind on the sidewalk, Mia stomped into the house.

"What was that all about?" her father asked.

"Ella brags," said Mia. "I don't want to play with her anymore."

Mia's dad reached out to put his arm around her.

"Why do you think she suddenly started bragging?" her dad asked.

"I don't know," said Mia. "But she's no fun."

"You know that Ella's mom is very, very sick," Mia's dad

explained. "Her mom can't come outside anymore and watch her ride her bike or play. Maybe Ella is just looking for someone to say, 'Good job.'"

Mia hadn't thought about why her friend was showing off. Mia only knew it wasn't fun to be around her.

"Ella might be upset that her mom is so sick and that she won't get better," said her dad. "How can you be a good friend for her?"

What do you think Mia said?

Let's Talk

What does it mean to brag? Why didn't Mia want to be around Ella? Who is your best friend?

Parent Connection

Young children are self-centered and crave attention. That's why they frequently say, "Watch me!" and "Look at me!" As children grow older, they become socially sensitive. They also learn to be aware of how others react to them. An older child who consistently displays attention-getting behavior may find friends only among younger children who are not as socially astute or children on the fringe of social circles.

Bringing It Home

• Sometimes we do things that make us unlovable to other people, but God always loves us.

• Because everything good in our lives comes from God, we have no reason to boast, but every reason to be humble: Jesus died for us despite our sins (Romans 5:8).

Let's Remember

Give thanks to the LORD, for He
is good. Psalm 136:1

A Happy Heart

"Sam, you forgot to make your bed," called his mom.

"Sorry, Mom," he said, racing up the stairs to the bedroom. He pulled up the covers, smoothed the pillows, and then put his green dinosaur on top. *Looks good,* he thought, and headed downstairs.

"Sam, could you sweep the kitchen?" asked his mom.

"Sure, Mom," said Sam. He got the broom and dustpan from the closet, then started sweeping. He swept under all the chairs and worked his way down the hall. Then he dumped out the dirt and put the cleaning tools back in the closet.

Sam was heading back upstairs to play when his dad came in from the garage.

His dad said, "Sam, would you help me clean out the car? We want it to look nice for Grandma."

Sam smiled and trotted out to the driveway. He was so happy his grandmother was coming that he planned to smile the whole day.

Dear God,

I'm happy about so many things. I'm happy because You love me and so does _____. I'm happy because _____. I'm happy because of Jesus. In His name. **Amen.**

Let's Talk

Why was Sam happy? What do you do to get ready for company? When have you smiled through a whole day?

Parent Connection

Looking back on childhood, we often recall happy memories, and that's good. Most children do not have major problems that darken the early years. Yet, learning to cope with jealousy, competition, fears, and uncertainty can be issues during the relatively carefree childhood years. However, even if a child is forced to survive challenging situations, he will feel empowered to face problems with major consequences in the future.

Bringing It Home

- God smiles when a child learns to love Him.
- We can be happy because Jesus died and rose for us.

Let's Remember

He [the Lord] made the moon
to mark the seasons.
Psalm 104:19

Moo in the Sky

"Moo," said baby Morgan, pointing to the window.

Grandma looked outside, then shook her head. "We can't see the moon from here," she said. "Let's try another window."

Caden watched to see where Grandma was taking his sister.

Grandma carried the baby into the kitchen and pulled open the shade. "Moo," said Morgan, looking out. Grandma looked all around, then shook her head.

"We can't see the moon from here either," she said. "Let's try another window."

This time, Caden followed them.

"Moo," said baby Morgan, pointing up through the front room window. "Moo, moo."

"Yes, Morgan," Grandma said. "There's the moon."

Caden asked, "Why does Morgan say 'moo' instead of 'moon'?"

"Morgan is just learning to talk," Grandma explained. "When you were a baby, you called me 'Amma.' You couldn't say 'Grandma' yet."

Caden thought about that. He wondered what else he said when he was little.

Dear God,

Thank You for helping me to grow up. I pray to You in Jesus' name.
Amen.

Let's Talk

What were the first words you learned to say? Since you were a baby, what is one thing you've learned to do with your feet? with your hands?

Let's Remember
Even a child makes himself known
by his acts. Proverbs 20:11

The Toy Box

Bam! Bam! Bam!

Natalie pounded the hammer.

"Good job, Honey," said Grandpa. "You hit the nail on the head."

Natalie giggled. She hoped to finish the project today, but the toy box still needed a lot of work. Two more nails would finish the construction part, and then they could paint.

Bam! Bam! Bam!

"Okay, now. This will be the last nail," said Grandpa.

Bam! Bam! Bam!

Natalie pulled off her goggles.

"I won't need the goggles to paint," she said.

"That's right," said Grandpa. He shook the paint can, then lifted off the lid. Natalie smiled when she saw the color. It would be perfect for her puppy's toy box.

Let's Talk

Were you surprised that Natalie was building a toy box for her pet? What color do you think Natalie chose? What kinds of toys would a puppy like?

Dear God,

Thank You for people who spend time with me. Thank You especially for _____. In Jesus' name. **Amen.**

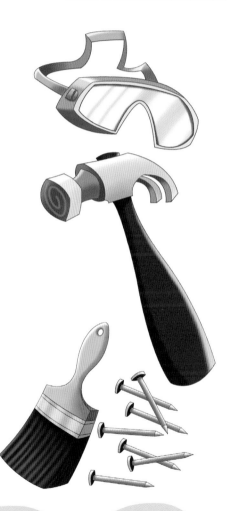

Bringing It Home

- Jesus said that when we show kindness to someone else, it's the same thing as showing kindness to Him (Matthew 25:40).

- The best way Jesus shows kindness is that He forgives all our sins and promises us a life in heaven.

Tickle Toes

Skippy walked into the bedroom, wagging his fluffy tail from side to side. He headed toward the bed and sniffed at the toes peeking out from under the covers. Nicholas giggled.

Skippy nuzzled his toes. Nicholas laughed out loud, then reached down to pet the large, furry animal.

"Skippy, we should call you 'Tickle Toes,'" Nicholas said. Skippy looked up, then woofed.

Mom called, "Nicholas, are you all tucked in? Ready for bed?"

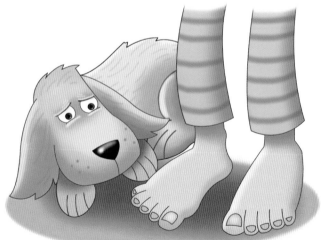

Parent Connection

A child's pet is quickly adopted as a member of the family. But for a child, a pet becomes more than a mere animal. A pet becomes a friend. Even if a child can't ride a two-wheeler or read a book, a dog or a cat will offer enjoyment. As a child cares for his pet, he learns to give and receive unconditional love. A household animal enriches a child's life and is a true blessing from God.

"Almost, Mom," Nicholas called back. "I'm playing with Tickle Toes."

Mom walked into the bedroom. "Tickle Toes?" she asked.

"Skippy," Nicholas explained. "He keeps tickling my feet, so I called him 'Tickle Toes.'"

"He's a wonderful dog," said Mom. "Perhaps tonight you can thank God for pets."

"Especially Tickle Toes," laughed Nicholas.

Let's Talk

Is "Tickle Toes" a good name for the dog? How did Nicholas feel when his dog tickled him? Where are you ticklish?

Bringing It Home

- God gives us pets as a reminder of His love.
- Jesus is God's best gift of love.

Let's Remember

Forgive, and you will be forgiven.
Luke 6:37

A Mystery

"Olivia!" called Mom. "Come see what I found."

Olivia ran to the kitchen. "What?" Olivia asked.

"What do you see here?" asked her mom, pointing to the glass patio door.

Olivia stared through the glass. She could see the barbecue grill and the umbrella table on the patio. Her swing set was in the backyard. A skinny little tree gave a bit of shade. Nothing looked out of place.

"I don't see anything different," said Olivia.

"I wiped the windows so they'd be clean when company comes, but look at that," said Mom. She pointed to a spot on the door.

"That's a print," said Olivia. "That's not mine, though. It's a paw print. I think Fluffy jumped up."

Taking Olivia's hand, Mom gently placed it on the door print. Olivia's hand perfectly matched the print on the door.

"The print is the same size as your hand," said her mom.

Olivia thought for a moment.

"No, Fluffy did it. I saw her," said Olivia.

"Well, Fluffy can't help clean the door, but you can," said Mom. "Which do you want to do? Spray the window or wipe it clean?"

Dear God,

When I make a mistake, I say, "I'm sorry." I know You will always forgive me. Through Jesus alone. Amen.

Let's Talk

The title of this story is "A Mystery." Was there really a mystery in this story? Why did Olivia blame Fluffy for the print?

Parent Connection

Admitting guilt is not easy for a child. Like adults, young quick-thinkers often shift the blame. Reminding a child he is forgiven makes it easier for a child to honestly admit his mistake. This is an important step in learning to be responsible for his actions.

Bringing It Home

• When we lie to cover up a sin, God forgives both sins because of Jesus.

• Jesus went to the cross carrying a heavy load: our sin.

Let's Remember

When the bow is in the clouds, I will see it and remember the everlasting covenant between God and every living creature. Genesis 9:16

A Bow in the Sky

Noah looked out the window. Rain ran down the window. But it didn't look like any new rain was falling in the puddles.

"Grandma, the rain is over," Noah called. He could hardly wait to get outside and splash in the big puddles.

Grandma came into the room. She peered out the window. The sky was not as dark. The rain had stopped.

"Noah, I think you're right," she said. "I know you want to get outside. I'll come too. The ground will be soft enough to pull some of those weeds."

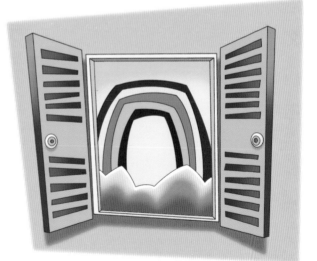

Dear God,

A rainbow is Your promise that You'll never flood the earth again. I know You keep Your promises. I know You keep Your promise to always love me. Through Jesus alone. **Amen.**

Noah tugged on his rain boots. Grandma collected her garden tools. Closing the front door, Grandma checked the sky again.

"Noah, look!" she said. "Look at God's promise."

Noah looked up. Grandma pointed to the colorful arch that stretched across the sky.

"Just like after the big flood with the first Noah," he said, smiling.

Let's Talk

Why was Noah eager to get outside? What did both the boy in this story and the Noah in the Bible see in the sky?

Parent Connection

Keeping our promise to our child is one way to gradually teach him that he can trust us. That's why it's important to promise only what we control or what will definitely happen. If there is any uncertainty, it's better to include an exit clause. For example, say, "I'll try to read an extra story" instead of "I promise I'll read an extra story." A promise is a word of honor that reflects a commitment, like God's promise reflected in the rainbow.

Bringing It Home

- The rainbow is God's promise that He will never again destroy the earth by flood.

- The most important promise God kept was to send a Savior to the world.

Standing Tall

Owen stood as straight and tall as he could. His mom stuck a piece of tape on the doorframe, right at the top of his head.

"All right, Kaylee," said Mrs. Jenkins. "Your turn."

Kaylee stood as straight and tall as she could. Owen's mom stuck a piece of tape on the doorframe, right at the top of her head.

Then Kaylee turned around to look at the door. The two pieces of tape were stuck on the same spot!

"You're both the same height," said Owen's mom.

"But I'm bigger," said Owen, sticking out his stomach.

"Do you want to stand on a scale to see who weighs more?" asked his mom.

"Let's do it," said Owen, heading for the bathroom closet.

Owen set the scale on the floor, then stepped on it. They all peered at the number.

Then Kaylee stood on the scale. They all waited for a number to appear.

"See?" said Owen. "I'm bigger than you."

Dear God,

I know it isn't important to You how big or tall I am. I know You love me, and that's what counts.
In Jesus' name. Amen.

Let's Talk

Why do you think Owen wanted to be bigger than Kaylee? Does it matter which child is taller or heavier?

Parent Connection

We tell children, "Don't be prideful," but we sometimes make that same mistake ourselves. Although we know it's wrong, we might be tempted to put other people down to build ourselves up. Yet, if we look for the good in others, we will not only model the biblical virtue of humility, but we will gain friends who offer encouragement for our parenting journey.

Bringing It Home

• Regardless of how we think we compare with someone else, none of us is perfect: we need the forgiveness Jesus offers.

• We receive God's love because of Jesus' work on our behalf.

Let's Remember

Let heaven and earth praise Him.
Psalm 69:34

Sky-High Beauty

Peyton shielded her eyes from the sun as she scanned the sky.

"I don't see anything," she said.

Her whole family waited and watched from the highest hill in the park. Right now, all they could see was a bright blue sky and fluffy white clouds.

Peyton's little brothers were bored. They started chasing each other and whiffing dandelions in the air.

But Peyton still watched the sky.

"There! Look over there," her father said, pointing. The dot in the sky got bigger. Now Peyton could see striped colors. The hot-air balloon floated closer, still high in the sky. Peyton's little brothers stopped running and looked up too.

"I see another one," said Peyton.

They all watched balloons from the festival float closer. Passengers in one of the baskets waved from up above. Peyton and her family waved back. All too soon, the balloons drifted away. Finally, the last balloon was just a speck in the sky.

"I wish hot-air balloons would fly over us every day," said Peyton. "They are so beautiful!"

Dear God,

I pray to You in Jesus' name. I love beautiful things. I especially like _____. Thank You, God, for the many pretty things You put in our world. **Amen.**

Let's Talk

In the first book of the Bible, we read that God made the heavens on the second day of Creation (Genesis 1:6–8). On which day did God make flowers that you smell? the stars that twinkle at night? animals to pet?

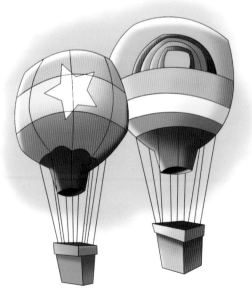

Let's Remember

I praise You for I am fearfully and
wonderfully made.
Psalm 139:14

The Right Size

James and Ryan squeezed into the closet. They were measuring themselves next to the ruler taped on the doorframe.

"See, I'm taller," said James.

"No," said Ryan. "Look at me."

He stretched his hands above his head, reaching high on the measuring stick.

"That's no fair!" said James as he moved into the kitchen. He thought for a moment, then said, "I can take bigger steps than you."

James stretched out his legs and took giant steps all around the room. Ryan tried that too, but he stretched out too far and he fell.

"What are you doing, boys?" asked Ryan's mom when she saw Ryan on the floor.

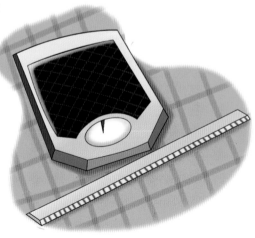

"We're seeing who's bigger," Ryan answered.

"You can also weigh who's heavier," said his mom.

"Yeah!" said Ryan. "Let's do it!"

The boys raced off.

What were they going to use to weigh themselves?

Let's Talk

What did the boys use to measure how tall they were? Who is the tallest person you know?

Parent Connection

Comparisons, some with an undercurrent of competition, frequently emerge in play situations. Informal observations naturally teach a child that God makes children in different colors, sizes, and shapes. Although children are quick to note differences, they often need adult guidance to notice similarities among people.

Bringing It Home

- God calls us His child, regardless of our age.
- A Christian parent is called to help a child grow up with knowledge of Jesus as our Savior and Redeemer.

Let's Remember

As one whom his mother comforts,
so I will comfort you. Isaiah 66:13

Cheer Up

Tears ran down Sarah's face. She had left her favorite doll outside overnight. It had rained. Now her doll's hair was wet and stringy. The beautiful pink gown stuck to her body. Her slipper had fallen off, so she had one bare foot. Sarah's favorite doll was ruined.

She was still crying when Thomas looked through the back fence. He unlatched the gate and ran into the yard.

"What's wrong?" he asked.

"My doll is ruined," Sarah sobbed.

Thomas looked at the bedraggled doll that hung limply from Sarah's hand. The doll looked awful.

Dear God,

When my friends are upset, show me how to help them feel better. Knowing You love me makes me feel _____. I pray to You in Jesus' name. Amen.

Thomas put his arm around Sarah. He said, "Do you want to play with my truck? I'll share my favorite dump truck."

Sarah just shook her head.

Let's Talk

How would you help Sarah feel better? When you are upset, who comforts you?

Parent Connection

When a child makes a mistake, she is often punished. But in this story, the child has already been punished by her forgetfulness. Often a parent is tempted to add a punishment "to teach a lesson." However, there is a big difference between punishment and discipline. Punishment only temporarily stops misbehavior. Discipline, which means "to teach or guide," teaches a child what to do instead.

Bringing It Home

- If we love God, we will be encouraging and supportive of others.
- Jesus died on the cross to forgive all the sin of all the world.

Let's Remember

Lord, teach us to pray. Luke 11:1

A Quick Prayer

"I'm too tired to pray," Michael mumbled, settling into his pillow.

"We've had a busy day," agreed his mom. "But we want to thank God for His blessings."

"You do it," said Michael, shifting the pillow under his head.

"Okay. We'll make it an echo prayer," said his mom.

"What's that?" Michael asked, opening his eyes.

"You say the words after me," said his mom. "I'll say, 'Thank You, God,' and you repeat. Now say, 'Thank You, God.'"

"Thank You, God," said Michael.

"For the fun I had playing hide-and-go-seek."

"For the fun I had playing hide-and-go-seek," said Michael.

"And for seeing Grandma."

"And for seeing Grandma," said Michael. "But pray faster, Mommy. Pray faster. God might be tired too."

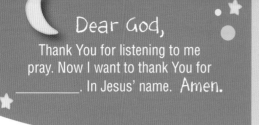

Dear God,

Thank You for listening to me pray. Now I want to thank You for _____. In Jesus' name. Amen.

Let's Talk

The Bible says God always listens to our prayers. Do you think God ever sleeps? When do you talk with God?

Parent Connection

Prayer is a conversation with God. A child experiences the truth of that fact when prayer is a normal part of the bedtime routine. When a child realizes that talking with God is as natural as talking to you, prayer is easily integrated into activities throughout the day.

Bringing it Home

- Communicating with God is so important that Jesus teaches us how to pray (Luke 11:1–13).

- God hears all our prayers to Him when we pray in Jesus' name.

Let's Remember

Oh, taste and see that the LORD is good.
Psalm 34:8

The Smell of Chocolate

Sean waited patiently for Grandma to open the box of candy. She tore off the wrapping, then lifted the lid. The smell of chocolate filled the air.

"Would you like a piece, Sean?" she asked.

"Oh, yes," said Sean.

"Take the one you touch," said his grandmother.

Sean studied the box. One piece looked like chocolate-covered peanuts. That would be all right, but what if those were raisins under the chocolate? Sean didn't like raisins, even when they were covered with chocolate.

Perhaps he should pick a round candy—but what if he got one with a pineapple or orange center? He liked a red center, but he couldn't see under the chocolate covering.

Square chocolates were usually caramels, but he didn't want his teeth to get all sticky.

"Well, Sean, do you see a piece you like?" Grandma asked.

"I don't know," Sean said, uncertain about which to choose.

"How about this one?" said Grandma, taking a candy cane off the Christmas tree.

"That is perfect," said Sean. "I can see what's inside, and I *love* peppermint."

Let's Talk

Why didn't Sean take a piece of candy from the box? How was a candy cane different from the chocolate in the box?

Be a Whale

"Smile," the photographer said.

Autumn couldn't just smile. She simply had to laugh! The rabbit that popped out from behind the camera and then suddenly flew across the room was just plain silly.

"That's a great shot," the photographer said. "We're all done."

Autumn carefully stepped around the big cloth that was draped over the stool.

After looking at the pictures, Autumn and her mom left the studio and headed for the food court.

"Honey, you looked so happy in the pictures," said her mom. "Why did you get upset with me this morning?"

"I didn't know what to do with my mad," Autumn said.

"It's not bad to be mad," said her mom. "When I'm angry, I blow it out. Look."

Autumn and her mom moved to the side of the walkway and stopped for a moment. Autumn watched as her mom took a deep breath and then blew out the air.

"When I get angry, I breathe and blow three times," her mom said.

In and out. In and out. In and out. They stood there in the mall, blowing air in and out.

"I'm like a whale spouting air," said Autumn.

"That's a great way to think about it," said her mom, smiling. "Next time you feel mad, act like a whale."

Let's Talk

What makes you mad? Do you think blowing like a whale when you're mad is a good idea?

Parent Connection

A child can be scared by the intensity of her own anger. In this story, Autumn describes a situation that many children face. Her mom suggests a good coping mechanism. Modeling ideas like this, even practicing coping strategies alongside a child, allows the child to express the feeling and effectively deal with it. So when you teach a child to count to 20, take a time-out, or talk through her feelings, a child gradually learns to cope.

Bringing It Home

- Anger is bad only when we allow the feeling to lead us into sinful thoughts, words, or actions.

- Because we are forgiven in Christ, we can turn anger into an opportunity for positive action, such as forgiving the person with whom we are angry.

A Busy Scene

Solomon listened intently. Yes, that was a siren. Fire trucks were his favorite. Perhaps today he'd see one.

Soon, a red pumper truck came tearing past the grocery store parking lot. More sirens blared. Tooting a horn for cars to move out of the way, a long hook-and-ladder truck drove down the street, then cautiously turned the corner.

Solomon sat quietly in the car, watching the truck pass and listening to other sirens in the distance. More trucks were on the way, and all other traffic was stopped until the emergency vehicles went by. Two blue-and-white police cars came from another direction, one after the other. An ambulance whizzed past; then a red-and-white fire chief's car followed a rescue truck.

Dear God,

Thank You for all the people who keep us safe. Thank You for police officers, ambulance drivers, and _____.
In Jesus' name. Amen.

Solomon's mom finished loading groceries into the car, then slammed the trunk shut.

"Mom, did you see the emergency vehicles?"

"I saw them and I heard them," his mom nodded. "Ready to pray?"

She climbed into the driver's seat and waited for Solomon to begin.

"Dear God, so many trucks drove past, there must be a big problem. Please send help to people who need it, and keep the firefighters safe. Amen."

Let's Talk

Solomon and his family stopped what they were doing to pray for people who needed help. They did this whenever they heard sirens. Why is this a good idea? How do you feel when you ask God to help others?

Parent Connection

The noise and fast-paced activity that accompanies emergencies can be overwhelming; a child might be thrilled by the excitement but scared by the uncertainty of the situation. Pausing to pray not only reminds a child that God is in control, but gives a child a constructive way to help.

Bringing It Home

- We pray in Jesus' name because Jesus talks to God on our behalf.

- God answers all our prayers in Jesus' name. He says yes; no; or wait, because He has something better in mind for us.

Let's Remember

Let us not grow weary of doing good.
Galatians 6:9

A Helpful Guy

Zachary and his mom were getting out of the car when they heard someone call, "Come back, Max!"

The sound came from down the street. Mr. Brady's dog, Max, had gotten loose. Soon the brown, floppy-eared animal was sniffing Zach's shoes and wagging his tail.

"Max, you get back here!" called Mr. Brady.

Max looked up, but then, with his leash trailing, he started running again.

Zach ran too, and he quickly grabbed the leash. Zach leaned down to pet the friendly dog and waited for Mr. Brady to reach them.

Parent Connection

During the first 10 years of parenting, we catch only glimpses that all our hard work is paying off. We savor the moments when a child independently reaches out to help someone. In this story, Zach not only felt good about helping, but was complimented by both his neighbor and his mom. A child who grows up in a culture of affirmation and acceptance will feel good about who he is and secure in the values by which he lives.

Panting, the elderly man said, "Thank you, Zach. I stopped to tie my shoe and I dropped the leash. I really appreciate you catching Max."

Zach smiled. He felt good inside, the same kind of feeling he had that morning when he made his bed without a reminder. Giving Max one more pat on the head, Zach ran back to the car.

His mom said, "Zach, that was really nice of you to help like that."

Let's Talk

Whom did Zach help? He knew that it feels good to do nice things. In what ways are you helpful to others?

Bringing It Home

- The love of Jesus is so wide and deep, there is always enough to share with others.

- Our obedience to God is a response to His love and mercy.

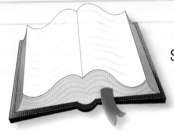

Let's Remember

Show perfect courtesy toward all people. Titus 3:2

A Mannerly Day

"Thanks, Miss Christy," said Thomas. He liked to play with James because his mom always had a snack ready for the boys.

"Thanks, Mom," said James.

"Two polite boys," said James's mom. "I appreciate your saying thank you."

"Thank you," said James and Thomas together. Laughing, the boys raced back to play. When James accidentally knocked over a garage Thomas was building, James said, "Sorry." And when Thomas picked up a car that had zoomed off the ramp, James said, "Thank you," and Thomas said, "You're welcome." Both boys were laughing when James's mom came through the room, carrying a laundry basket.

"Need help?" Thomas asked.

"Why, thank you, Thomas," said Miss Christy. "You certainly have good manners."

The boys laughed so hard, they fell on the floor.

Let's Talk

The boys thought it was silly that they had so many opportunities to be polite, but being courteous is a way to show respect. Who teaches you manners? Are you as polite as the boys in this story? When is it important to be polite?

Parent Connection

We teach young children to say "Please" and "Thank you," known by generations as "magic words." As children grow up, those terms can easily be forgotten, especially if we respond to demands or requests that don't include the magic words. A child may need to be prompted to practice courtesy, but when manners become learned behaviors, those lessons carry over for a lifetime.

Bringing It Home

- One way Jesus expressed His love for others was by teaching them and showing them compassion.

- We show respect for others because Jesus loved people enough to die for them.

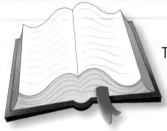

Let's Remember

The LORD your God will bless
you, as He promised you.
Deuteronomy 15:6

Tangled

"I'm all tangled up," said a muffled voice under the covers. "I can't get out."

"You really are twisted in the covers," said Mommy, trying to find Jacob under the sheet. First a foot appeared. Then Mom tugged on the sheet and uncovered a leg. Finally, all of Jacob popped out.

"Whew!" he said.

"What were you trying to do?" asked his mom.

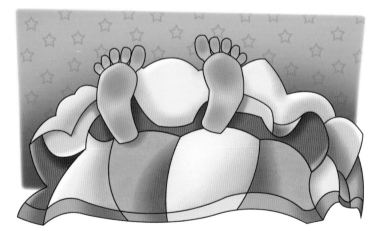

Dear God,

People all around the world read the Bible in their own language. I read it in my language, _____.

You understand every language. In Jesus' name. Amen.

"I was twisting my body into alphabet letters," Jacob said. "I did really well with the *J*. Watch."

Jacob curled his legs around to make the curvy part of the letter, then stretched out his arms to make the top of the *J*.

Laughing, his mom said, "Next time when you're playing with the alphabet in bed, try using your fingers."

Jacob thought for a moment, then said, "That's a good idea. If you play with me, we'll have 20 fingers to use. We can do the whole alphabet!"

Let's Talk

Would "Untangled" be a better title for this story? What letters can you make using your body? using only your fingers?

Bringing It Home

- God gave us the Bible as His true Word to us so we could learn about Jesus, our Redeemer.

- Each day, we can communicate the most important words in the world to a child: "Jesus loves you and so do I."

Let's Remember
God is love. 1 John 4:16

Peek-a-Boo Hearts

Tyler stepped out of the shower. Teeth chattering, he wrapped the towel tightly around his bare body.

"I'm cold," he said. "Get my pajamas."

"Do I hear a 'please'?" asked his dad.

"Please get my pajamas," Tyler said. Tyler said a fast "Thanks" as his dad helped him into the warm pjs.

Then Tyler reached up to the steamy bathroom mirror and drew a tiny heart with his finger in an empty corner of the glass. Hearts already showed through the fog on the rest of the mirror. Tyler stared at the mirror. Every night after his shower, he watched until the hearts faded away with the steam.

Little Visits AT BEDTIME

Parent Connection

Tracing a heart onto a steamy bathroom mirror can be an easy reminder of your love for each other and God's love for us all. Simple actions, like drawing hearts and crosses, remind a child that he is loved by God and you.

"Do you miss the hearts after they fade away?" asked his dad.

"Not really," said Tyler. "I know they are there, waiting to pop through the fog tomorrow."

Let's Talk

God's love is like shapes drawn on a foggy mirror: we can't always see His love, but we know it's there. How does God show that He loves you? What shape would you draw as a reminder that God loves you?

Bringing It Home

• Jesus showed love in big and small ways.

• God's love for us is so great that He sent His Son to die for us so we could be forgiven and have eternal life with Him.

Sleep Tight

Victoria reached up to feel her dad's whiskers as he tucked the covers around her. Then he stretched out on the floor and lay next to her bed, just as he did each night.

"Okay, Sweetheart," her dad said. "Let's talk about the day."

Victoria talked nonstop about the places she went and the people she saw. She talked about the food she ate, remembering the ice-cream cone with an extra scoop. Victoria told her dad all about the helicopter that had flown right over their house. She told him about the penny she found on the sidewalk.

Then she asked, "Daddy, why do you always lie down at night on the floor next to the bed?"

Daddy didn't answer. Listening, she heard a quiet snoring. Victoria sat up and peered over the edge of the bed.

What was her dad doing?

Dear God,

I pray to You in Jesus' name: Thank You for watching over me when I sleep. Good night, God. Amen.

Let's Talk

A routine is something you repeat again and again. What was Victoria's nighttime routine? What do you do each night before you go to sleep?

A Froggy Night

William looked out the window, but everything was covered with gray fog. He could barely see the light that usually shined brightly on the street below. The tall tree next to the house was only a dim, dark shadow.

"It's a froggy, froggy night," William told his dad.

"I believe it's a foggy, foggy night," corrected his father.

"No, I want to pretend it's a froggy night," said William. "Frogs are hopping through the mist."

William hopped around the room, saying, "*Ribbet, ribbet.*" His father laughed.

"It *sounds* like a froggy night, and it *looks* like a froggy night, but now it's time for all the frogs and all little boys to climb into bed."

"*Ribbet, ribbet,*" said William, and he hopped into bed.

Let's Talk

Why was "A Froggy Night" a good title for this story? Fog is like a cloud that settles on the ground. Which do you like better: a foggy day or a sunny day? Why?

Dear God,

I like snowy days because _____.
I like rainy days because _____. My
favorite weather is _____. Thank You
for hearing me in all kinds of weather.
In Jesus' name. Amen.

Parent Connection

Weather tracking is an easy way for a child to begin to understand the variety and scope of God's creation. During seasonal transitions, invite your child to draw a weather symbol each day on the family calendar. At the end of a month, your child can count the number of sunny, rainy, foggy, and cloudy days.

Bringing It Home

- The varieties of weather show the majesty and power of God as Creator of the universe.

- Jesus showed His power over the earth by calming the storm; He showed His power over sin, death, and the devil when He died on the cross, descended into hell, and rose on Easter.

Let's Remember

Let me hear joy and gladness.
Psalm 51:8

A Dog's Lunch

Wyatt's mom set a glass of milk on the table at the same time that he reached for it. "Whoops," she said, as the glass toppled over. Rusty, Wyatt's dog, quickly lapped up the spill.

His mom set another glass on the table, then turned around with a tray of steaming chicken nuggets. Wyatt grabbed one but dropped it immediately.

"Ouch! That's hot," he said, and the nugget fell to the floor. Rusty sniffed the nugget, then started pawing at it.

"Sorry, Honey," said his mom. "I should have warned you that it was still hot."

His mom cut open a couple of nuggets to cool. Then she reached for the salad, but she stumbled over Rusty, who was nibbling the nugget. Lettuce flew everywhere.

"Oh, no!" she said, laughing.

"What's funny?" asked Wyatt. "The milk spilled, the nuggets were burning hot, and there's lettuce all over the kitchen."

"I'm laughing because Rusty is the only one who's eating lunch," said his mom.

Dear God,

I smile whenever I think of Jesus as my Savior. That makes me feel ____. In Jesus' name. **Amen.**

Let's Talk

Do you think Wyatt started to laugh too? Is this story funny or sad?

Litter Bug

Zander watched as the other boy unwrapped his gum, tossed the wrapper onto the ground, then walked away.

"Mommy," he said, tugging at his mom's arm, "that boy just littered."

His mom slowed her bike to look where Zander pointed. A bit of wind lifted the shiny bit of paper, and it started to fly along the ground.

"Why didn't he look for a trash can?" Zander asked.

"I don't know," his mom answered. "There's a trash can and a recycling bin just inside the park gate."

"Or he could have put the scrap in his pocket and thrown it away when he got home," Zander said.

He was still frowning at the end of their ride, when they were putting away their bikes.

"Seeing someone litter really bothered you," said his mom. "Why are you so upset about that?" What do you think Zander said?

Dear God,

Thank You for creating such a beautiful world. Help me and others take good care of our earth. In Jesus' name. **Amen.**

Let's Talk

A person who fails to put trash in a trash can or recycle bin is sometimes called a "litterbug." Have you ever seen a litterbug? How should a litterbug be punished?

Parent Connection

Social historians credit children, perhaps like the child in this story, with playing a significant role in the "green revolution." Students have implemented at home many of the ideas learned in school; now, "Reduce, reuse, recycle" is only one element of eco-sensitivity. This expanded emphasis naturally flows from the thankfulness we feel to care for the earth God created.

Bringing It Home

• God gave us responsibility to be good stewards of the earth, and we honor Him by caring for it.

• God created the world as a special place for us, but His intention is for us to live forever with Him in heaven; Jesus makes it possible for that to happen.

Let's Remember

When You open Your hand,
they are filled with good things.
Psalm 104:28

Food Fun

"Cut out your sandwich with these cookie cutters," said Juan's grandma. "It's fun to eat something that looks a little different."

Jackson surveyed the cookie cutters lying on the kitchen counter. He liked the star, and the tree was nice too. But finally Jackson said, "I'm going to do something really different with my sandwich."

Juan watched as his friend pulled off long strips of string cheese. He nibbled a few pieces, then laid the leftover cheese strips on either side of the piece of bread.

"That's the hair," explained Jackson. Next he used a round cookie cutter to make a half-circle and two small circles of meat. He put these on top of the bread. With eyes and a mouth, the bread started to look like a person's face. Then he turned the mustard bottle upside down. Patiently, he waited for a single drop of mustard to drip, right in the center of the bread.

Juan studied his friend's sandwich.

"It's a happy face with long hair," explained Jackson.

"I want to do that too," said Juan.

Dear God,

Sometimes I forget to thank You for the food You give me. Thank You especially for my favorite lunch, which is _____. In Jesus' name. **Amen.**

Let's Talk

What did Jackson use to make his sandwich face? How do you think Jackson felt when his friend wanted to copy his idea? Have you ever made a face on a sandwich?

Parent Connection

If imitation is the sincerest form of flattery, then in this situation, Jackson received a major compliment. Young children are self-centered, so using words to give a compliment does not naturally happen. They model their compliments after those they receive and what they hear us tell others.

Bringing It Home

- God created us in His image, which means we are holy, like Him.

- God created us to be exactly who we are: His children, forgiven and redeemed through Jesus.

Let's Remember

Bless the LORD, all His works,
in all places of His dominion.
Psalm 103:22

A Circle Walk

Austin said, "I'm bored."

Riley said, "I'm bored too." It was too hot to play ball. They had used up their computer time for the day. They had no new books to read, and they weren't going swimming until later.

"What are you doing?" asked their mom.

"Nothing," said Austin.

"There's nothing to do," said Riley.

Their mom thought for a moment, then said, "Let's take a walk before it gets any hotter. Wait here. I'll be right back," she said.

She came out of the house carrying a long string and two empty bags. Then they started walking down the street. When they came to the corner, she spread the string in a circle under a tree.

"Let's see what we can find inside this circle," she said.

Riley picked up several broken bricks. He could use those with his dump truck. Austin collected different colored rocks.

They set up the circle at different places in the neighborhood. Then the two boys dragged home heavy bags. During lunch, they talked about the many things they were going to do with their treasures.

Dear God,

The world You created is full of neat stuff. Sometimes I forget to notice little things, like _____. Thank You, God, in Jesus' name. **Amen.**

Parent Connection
Statistics show that screen time continues to rise. It's tempting to use computer, television, video, or cell phone screens as babysitters. But before that happens next time, challenge yourself and your child to move beyond the screen. Consult online sites for ideas, if you wish, then leave the screen behind.

Their mother interrupted, saying, "What did you learn this morning?" What do you think they said?

Let's Talk

Why did the boys' mother bring string and two bags? When you are bored, what are three things you can do?

Bringing It Home

• Jesus is our best friend because He loves us more than anyone else does.

• When our sin breaks our friendship with God, Jesus' death restores the relationship.

Sleepytime

Now the light has gone away;
Father, listen while I pray,
Asking Thee to watch and keep
And to send me quiet sleep.

Jesus, Savior, wash away
All that has been wrong today;
Help me every day to be
Good and gentle, more like Thee.

Let my near and dear ones be
Always near and dear to Thee;
O bring me and all I love
To Thy happy home above. Amen.

(Public Domain)

Prayers

It's time for me to go to sleep.
Dear Jesus, now I pray:
Thank You, Lord, for all You've done.
And thank You for today. Amen.

(God's Children Pray)

Lord Jesus, keep me in Your sight
Through the coming hours of night.
Then when morning sunlight beams,
Wake me, Lord, from happy dreams. Amen.

(God's Children Pray)

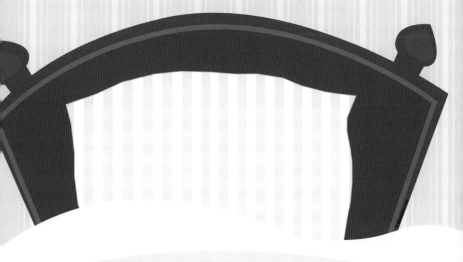

About the Author

An educator, corporate consultant, and media personality, Dr. Mary Manz Simon is an award-winning author whose books have sold more than three million copies in English. Her titles are available in ten languages. Also a popular national conference presenter, she speaks at events throughout the United States and Canada. She earned bachelor's, master's, and doctoral degrees in education. Her short-format radio program "Front Porch Parenting," which airs daily on 180 radio stations, offers "expert advice from a friendly shoulder." Mary is the mother of three and grandmother of four boys.

About the Little Visits® Series

For more than fifty years, Little Visits® books have been associated with family devotions that share the Gospel of Jesus Christ with children. Each book in the series reinforces scriptural truths and faith concepts centered on God's love for us in Christ Jesus. We hope this newest volume assists you in maintaining regular winding-down activities that you and your child will anticipate with pleasure and remember with joy.

Little Visits AT BEDTIME